Grace
IN YOUR SECOND ACT

A GUIDE TO AGING GRACEFULLY

FLORENCE LaRUE
WITH
JENNY PASCHALL

WESTBOW
PRESS®
A DIVISION OF THOMAS NELSON
& ZONDERVAN

WestBow Press books may be ordered through booksellers or by contacting:

WestBow Press
A Division of Thomas Nelson & Zondervan
1663 Liberty Drive
Bloomington, IN 47403
www.westbowpress.com
844-714-3454

Scripture quotations marked NKJV are taken from the New King James Version®. Copyright © 1982 by Thomas Nelson. Used by permission. All rights reserved.

ISBN: 978-1-6642-2708-8 (sc)
ISBN: 978-1-6642-2709-5 (hc)
ISBN: 978-1-6642-2707-1 (e)

Library of Congress Control Number: 2021904840

Print information available on the last page.

WestBow Press rev. date: 05/24/2021

To my mother, Sara LaRue, who was grace incarnate.

CONTENTS

"Thanks be to God for His indescribable gift."

—2 Corinthians 9:15

INTRODUCTION

I never felt beautiful. I was different. In a sea of White faces, I had brown skin, larger lips and frizzy hair and was raised in a different type environment from the other children. Although my hardworking, divorced mother bought me clothes that she could barely afford, that didn't help how I felt about my physical appearance. I wanted to be accepted and to blend in with the other children, and for some reason, I thought if I was pretty, this would happen. Why this focus on physical beauty? Perhaps because it seemed to me that all the happy and loved girls in the movies were beautiful (Heidi, etc.). Gram, as everyone called my grandmother, tried to instill in me that "Pretty is as pretty does." and that I was, indeed, beautiful.

It's often been suggested to me that I write a book on beauty, and my reply has always been "Why?" or "Why me?" I never thought I was a natural beauty and often didn't know how to gracefully accept the compliments I received on my appearance. I did enjoy experimenting with makeup to look my best—with the help of my friends "Miss Fashion Fair," "Ms. Maybelline," "Mr. Mac," and others! In addition, I have always liked creating my own style in dressing, and at the encouragement of my grandmother and mother, I worked hard to be spiritually and mentally beautiful. I also resisted writing about beauty because I didn't know what I could write that would be different from the many other books on the subject or what I could share that would make a positive difference and be helpful to those who would read it.

Several years ago, when the subject of writing a book was brought up again, I began to reflect upon the beauty contests I had won, when there were clearly young ladies more physically beautiful than I was. I thought of all the different ways I looked when people remarked favorably on my appearance. I realized there was never one particular look that drew compliments. Sometimes I was fully made up, and other times I was wearing absolutely no makeup at all. It finally dawned on me. It was not just my physical appearance people saw but also my attitude and the "light within me." I realized I received most compliments when I was in a positive mood. People were seeing my joy, my soul, my attitude, and my desire to live and not merely exist. It was then too that I realized beauty can be summed up in a four-letter word: *love*. Love of self and others, love of life, and most of all, love of God.

Haven't you noticed that you look your best when you are in love? So if you're in love with life every day, you'll look beautiful every day. I also perceived that there are three very important dimensions of beauty: physical, mental, and spiritual. So I conducted extensive research and asked people what they wanted to know about beauty. In general, I discovered that almost everyone I talked to wanted to know my beauty regimen. They came up with questions like "What do you eat?" "Do you exercise?" "What brand of makeup do you wear?" and "What is that extra something you have, because I want some of that?"

In this book, while answering these questions, I share with you my thoughts in a manner that I hope will not only be fun and informative but will also have helpful suggestions and information that will give you ideas to help you look and feel *your* best. I've included ideas to help you live a fulfilled, blessed, and happy life free to be yourself reaching for the destiny that God has for you.

I have the uncanny ability to see people not as they appear but to perceive the potential in them, be it physical appearance or talent. Do I take my own advice? Not always! But at least I have the information at my fingertips!

The principles on these pages are meant for people of all ages. Young people can benefit from beginning a life of good health at an early age so as to lead a more productive and fulfilling life. And more mature people will note that it is never too late to begin the journey toward reaching your potential in health and beauty! As Coco Chanel said, "You can be gorgeous at thirty, charming at forty, and irresistible for the rest of your life."

I want to stress that the information in this book is not about what action to take for instant beauty. There is much information readily available on "age-defying" and "beauty-enhancing" products and the best plastic surgeons for whatever procedure you desire! My goal in writing this book is to help you to free yourself to let *your* light shine—mentally, physically, and spiritually. Be the *you* that God meant you to be. Don't hide your light, which represents the talents and gifts God has given you. Use it. Let it shine.

Chapter 1

EMBRACE AGING

> So much has been said and sung of beautiful young girls, why
> doesn't someone wake up to the beauty of old women?
>
> —Harriet Beecher Stowe

Aging is something that happens to everyone. In fact, it happens to every living thing. We can't avoid aging, but we can choose *how* to age. Do you want to age gracefully, or would you prefer to fight it all the way? I have decided to enjoy each season. If you have less energy, adjust your life accordingly. Live. Don't just exist. I am so grateful to God for allowing me to continue having experiences that give me the wisdom to handle things that happen in my life. Wisdom helps us all to help others who may be going through something we've already experienced.

In 1900, the average life expectancy was forty-seven years old! That seems extraordinary now, when the life expectancy for a woman is about eighty-one years, and more and more people are living past one hundred. Baby boomers are rewriting the rules of aging. Often people will ask me my age and then say, "Oh, you don't look it." Well, guess what. This is what *my* age looks like! Take a look at yourself in the mirror. This is what *your* age looks like. Numbers are irrelevant. It's what looks back at you that counts. Don't pretend to be younger. Instead, celebrate being older. Be proud. If you have lines, you've earned them. If you have a few extra pounds, you're allowed to. At twenty you had a youthful, dewy glow. Now you have an inner light that shines through. You've weathered storms and become fearless. Look upon this stage of your life as another exciting experience. Maybe you can't wear the same cinched belts and six-inch heels (or maybe you can, in which case, enjoy!), but this is a time to be authentic and draw from all that knowledge you've filed away over the years.

We have to stop buying into the myth that the only people who matter are the young. Create your own image and defy the stereotype. We don't have to be invisible just because we're older. We can wear the clothes we couldn't afford or didn't have the courage to wear before. We can go to places that once scared us. Enjoy the freedom that comes with your new age.

I've been blessed to travel all over the world. I've noticed that countries have very different attitudes toward aging. When I was in Japan, for example, it was clear that older people are revered for their wisdom. Interestingly, the elderly are more active too. I saw people in their seventies and eighties walking great distances—far more than would be normal here in the United States. I don't know if it was their diet, their mindset, or both, but it fascinated me. Style-wise, older women in France and Italy are more fashionable without trying to look like teenagers. They're elegant and not frightened of being desirable. They're very comfortable in their skin—even if it's a bit lined! Neither sex seems to be as worried about their age. Women are beautiful, feminine, and ageless. And European men treat them as though they're attractive. Harmless flirting is a more European habit, and it's one I rather like. It makes a woman know that the time and effort she's put into her appearance is appreciated.

Looking back, I realize that aging must have been very difficult for my mother. She was divorced and bringing up four daughters as a single parent, and then she developed cancer, so she really had a great many challenges in her life.

I have very few regrets, but among them are that I would have spent more time with family, I would have taken more risks in my career, and I would have finished this book sooner!

Grace in Our Second Act

An often quoted saying is "Don't regret growing older. It's a privilege denied to many." And isn't that the truth? How many people do we all know who never reached an age when they could complain about their wrinkles or have to search for those elusive reading glasses when they know they just put them down a minute ago?

For that reason alone, we have to embrace aging with grace and thankfulness. In fact, there are numerous reasons why our second act should be one of the happiest times of our lives. Studies have shown that older people typically have less stress. We don't worry about work so much (if we're not already retired), relationships are steadier and less demanding, we have learned better coping skills, and we have more balanced perspectives when we do have to deal with problems.

"The Harvard Study of Adult Development," which tracked participants into their eighties and nineties, found that lifestyle factors have a bigger impact on happiness levels than wealth or fame. In addition, "subjective health" (how healthy you feel) has a greater impact than "objective health" (whether or not you have health issues). In other words, you're only as old as you feel! Many over sixty-five now say they feel younger than their age.

Of course, we all have physical setbacks sometimes, but that doesn't mean we shouldn't continue to focus on the positive. I have had two hip replacement surgeries but performed after both. I wasn't able to dance around the stage at first but I cheered myself (and my audience) by having a fantastic bling-covered cane as my accessory for a few performances. It's important to adapt to any changes that may occur, be flexible, and maintain a positive attitude.

The theme of this book is grace in your second act. I've mentioned many ways in which we can embrace aging—physically, mentally, and spiritually. It seems to be something that is more difficult for some than others. For example, Frank Lloyd Wright, the famous architect, said, "The longer I live, the more beautiful life becomes." Clearly, aging was something he accepted with grace and joy. However, the talented and funny writer Nora Ephron had a more difficult time. In her best-selling book *I Feel Bad about My Neck*, she wrote this: "The honest truth is that it's sad to be over sixty." Two hugely talented people, two very different perspectives.

If you expect to be old and helpless, you will be! Life's not over until God says it's over.

Physical Grace

In our age-conscious society, aging is near the top of the list of beauty concerns. It is amazing what Americans will do to appear young. In many cultures, the elderly are respected for their wisdom. I find it amazing that in American society we spend millions of dollars to prevent death and then are ashamed to admit that God has allowed us to live beyond the age of thirty-nine! We must remember that no one of is growing younger. We also tend to forget that there is a difference in getting "old" and growing "older." Cheese gets old. I desire to grow older!

"What's the difference?" you ask. To me, getting old conjures up the picture of a stagnant person who has no dreams or goals and has given up on life. Whereas a person who grows older continues to live and not merely exist. Even when signs of aging creep up, he or she still keeps active. He or she still thinks of ways to help others and be a productive citizen, which could mean babysitting for a single parent, helping at church or synagogue, or doing community service by phone if the body is weak.

When talking of the physical aspects of grace in your second act, I suppose I should address cosmetic surgery. Personally, I think it's ridiculous to see a man or woman who looks twenty but can't walk a mile or is too weak to enjoy physical activities like dancing. What good is it to look young but not be able to enjoy the pleasures of youthful living? Now I'm not saying I'm against having cosmetic surgery. I say if the idea feels good and you can afford a reputable doctor, go for it. But be sensible. Know that you are still the same age in your heart and mind. And cosmetic surgery should not change your friends' attitudes toward you. It may help you attract a mate, but it's what's inside that counts. That's what will help keep your mate! As a matter of fact, I suggest you do a little surgery to your thinking before the surgery to your face or body. If that little tummy is going to upset your significant other that much, I'd think twice! True love overlooks those little flaws!

Of course, it's sometimes tough to look in the mirror, expecting to see your younger self but that older person is staring back at you instead. It's very difficult for some women to let go of their younger selves. We want to look like we used to. The way to deal with that is not to change your face but to change your mindset. Very few of us would turn the clock back if it meant we'd lose the wealth of experience we've gained or have to revisit difficult times when we underestimated our own value. Learn to love the new you, and stop caring about what other people are seeing on the surface. We all see those aging celebrities who are clinging desperately to their youth, looking far less attractive than those who have embraced the new version of themselves. The seventy-year-old supermodel Lauren Hutton is a perfect example of a woman who has accepted aging and who celebrates her mature beauty.

It isn't just our faces that no longer resemble our younger selves. Our bodies have changed too. I don't like slowing down and not being able to physically do some of the things I did when I was younger. I'm sometimes frustrated by the physical limitations that come with aging, like having hip replacements. I wore mine out by dancing and being so active. Sometimes I wonder if I could have done something to take better care of myself earlier. I haven't had a cold in years, so I know I've done something right in terms of caring for my immune system. The most important aspect of aging for me is the knowledge that I have less time to do some of the things I would like to do. I'm very aware of time. That's one of the few things we can't buy more of.

Mental Grace

Life is a beautiful journey of discovery. An inevitable part of that is growing older, so let's once and for all stop this pursuit for eternal youth! Don't fight aging. Embrace it! Youth isn't necessarily the ideal state. Yes, of course, it's great to be young. But oh, the pain and angst we all went through before we had the life experiences that shaped us and made us the people we are today. From zits to boyfriends, job interviews, college papers, falling in and out of love, being too fat or too thin, having babies, worrying about whether people liked us, and agonizing about whether we could actually do the job we were being paid to do, the list is endless. All those sleepless nights worrying about things that somehow, magically, got sorted out. I guarantee if we were confronted with those problems now, we'd shrug our shoulders, laugh, and agree we wasted too much precious time sweating the small stuff.

We live in a society that constantly reinforces the negative aspects of aging. But there's no way we can stop that clock from ticking. Aging gracefully isn't always easy, but we can help ourselves if we have the right attitude. The saddest thing for me is when I meet people who are filled with regrets for all the things they didn't do. Unfortunately, there are no redos in this life, so it's best to acknowledge your mistakes and learn from them rather than dwelling on them and becoming sad and possibly even bitter. Be proud of your achievements. Positive feelings are much healthier for your mental and physical well-being.

It's important to remember that older people are survivors. By the time most of us reach middle age, we've been through quite a lot. Among other things, we've had broken hearts, disappointments, health issues, and bereavements. Many of us have had children and careers, with all the ups and downs they both bring. We've ridden the roller coaster of emotions, from unimaginable joy to deep sadness. And we've survived it all.

One very important part of mental grace is to accept that aging changes everyone. Believe it or not, you're not the exception!

You have to continue to find things that bring you joy and challenge your mind. Whether it's travel, hobbies, spiritual pursuits, or spending time with family and friends, there's no reason why you can't fill your days with happy and stimulating experiences. Keep busy, and stay curious. Don't allow yourself to get into a rut mentally. Old dogs can learn new tricks! So don't dwell on the negatives of aging. Embrace the fact that you now have resilience, wisdom, and a mature outlook. What a powerful combination.

Chapter 2

ATTITUDE

A happy woman is one who has no cares at all; a cheerful woman
is one who has cares but doesn't let them get her down.

—Beverly Sills

You might ask, "What does attitude have to do with beauty?" And I answer, "Everything!" The way *you* think about *you* really affects what others think about you. If you act old, you'll look old. The actress Helen Mirren said about aging, "I don't look so good, but I don't care." Now I'm sure she does care because she always looks fantastic, so she clearly pays attention to her appearance. But the way she has embraced aging has given her a terrific, relaxed attitude, which makes her extremely attractive and engaging.

Why is it that, some years ago when Sophia Loren was seventy-two years of age, she scored higher in an online poll to identify the world's most naturally beautiful woman than one popular thirtysomething-year-old actress? Ms. Loren noted love of life as one of her beauty secrets! She has a positive attitude, which gives her an extraordinary inner glow. It's important to block out the constant subliminal pro-youth message. Many of those flawless models in the glossy ads look surprisingly ordinary before their photos are airbrushed and edited. Perfection is a myth!

Are you confident with your appearance? Do you have to check yourself in every mirror you pass? Let's face it. Most people want to be thought of as attractive, and if we don't feel beautiful, we waste time doing everything we can to achieve that goal. I know. I've done it! Trying to change my look with makeup, wearing ridiculous hairstyles, squeezing myself into clothes that were too tight or too short—I'm sure most of us have done the same. And what a waste of time it all is.

It's been said that everything begins in the mind. How and what you think about yourself has a direct effect on your appearance. Think about it. How many people have you ever heard say they were satisfied with their appearance? Most people complain about their weight, their hair (too curly or too straight!) their height, or some other physical characteristic that they are unhappy with. Few people point out their good features or thank God for their good physical and/or mental health.

Now if you want to make sensible changes in your appearance, go ahead. But until you reach your goal, enjoy who you are. For instance, while you work on losing or gaining a few pounds, enjoy the fact that you have beautiful hair, flawless skin, or whatever your good features are. (Yes, we all have at least one! Don't be so hard on yourself.) When I gain a few unwanted pounds, I dress to camouflage it and accentuate the fact that I have naturally good skin. I have some lovely black dresses and pants that I purchased when I gained a little weight, and they look chic no matter what I weigh, so I wear them with flair and feel great. When my hair doesn't look its best, I simply wear a hairpiece or a hat and instantly feel glamorous.

I'm sure you've seen plump women with slim, athletic husbands or a quite plain woman with a stunningly handsome man. Those women are beautiful in their husbands' eyes, and they are probably confident with their appearance.

Most of us have heard the expression "Beauty is in the eyes of the beholder." This expression is true, but it is influenced by the culture in which one lives: the extremely large buttocks that are thought attractive in some cultures are not considered so in others. Small hips were once thought desirable in the United States, but now that's changing. Think of the torture some women around the world and through the ages have endured to be considered beautiful: stretching their necks into disfiguring lengths, binding their feet so they will remain child sized all their life, starving themselves (sometimes to the point of death) to be thin, etc. Our thinking has really changed and continues to evolve daily, largely influenced by the latest movie star or popular celebrity, but women still go to drastic lengths to acquire society's current ideal of beauty.

Women in the United States are particularly sensitive about their weight. It is their number one complaint. And that's something that the majority of them can do something about if they choose. Notice I said "if they choose." Most of them don't want to do the work of exercising, sacrificing their favorite calorie-laden foods to lose weight, or planning a healthy diet to gain weight. I know that isn't you or you wouldn't be reading this book, but I can't tell you how many times I have had an overweight woman sit next to me eating her french fries and hamburger and drinking her large Coke and say to me, "Girl, how do you stay so small?" while she watches me eat my salad. You have to reeducate your mind to a new way of thinking. When you eat anything, ask yourself if what you're eating is going to nourish you or harm you. And by *harm,* I mean put on you harmful fat that will damage your heart. Or will it nourish your organs and put muscle on your body? It really is a mind thing.

I admit I've been caught up in the thin syndrome, weighing myself every day to maintain a certain weight. Fortunately, as a child and well into my adult years, I could eat as much of anything I wanted and not gain an ounce. I attribute this partly to heredity and partly to the fact that I was always very active.

During my first ten years as a member of The 5th Dimension, I weighed around 110 pounds and wore a size 2. Then as the years progressed, I gained weight until I reached my present weight of 120 pounds, and I wear a size six or eight. I feel that my ideal weight at my mature age is between 115 and 125 pounds. I'm very muscular, and muscle weighs more than fat. I weighed 110 pounds when I was experiencing some grief, and everyone told me I looked sick. But I really don't care what I weigh as long as my size six clothes fit *well* and don't cry out, "Get a size eight!"

You see, I finally learned to accept myself as I am, especially those things I cannot change. I'm not going to grow any taller, and no matter how much weight I lose or gain, I'm still going to have the same body type. God didn't make any mistakes. I am happier when I just try to be the best Florence I can be—mentally, physically, and spiritually. I'm healthy and happy, and there is no other person like me—or like you!

But attitude isn't just about your looks. It's how you project yourself in every way. Think about what lifts your spirits. If you can surround yourself with people and possessions that make you feel good—valued family members and friends, items that please you like flowers, and treasured memorabilia—your attitude will be more positive. Of course, being a mother and grandmother, my family will always give me that surge of happiness. I often listen to old phone messages from my son saying, "Hi, Mom. I just called to say I love you." Or my grandson saying, "Hi, Granny. I miss you *so* much!" That always warms my heart and lifts my spirits!

Friends can be a very important part of your attitude. It helps to have one or two good friends who will help to keep you mentally grounded, who will be honest and tell you the truth, no matter if it's when you dye your hair red and it looks terrible or whether you're behaving unreasonably. I have several "sisters in the Lord" with whom I am so connected that when I am going through something, one of them will call, not even knowing the situation! I'm also blessed to have several friends I may not see or talk to for a long time, but they're there when I need them! On the other hand, you may benefit from eliminating some negative people from your life or spending less time around them.

GIGO (garbage in, garbage out) is a computer science acronym that implies bad input will result in bad output. That can also apply very well to television. TV is often misused as a babysitter or to waste time filling one's mind with unnecessary crime and violence. But there are some programs that are mentally stimulating or soothing to the mind. For stimulation and encouragement, I like to watch people like Joyce Meyer, T. D. Jakes, Joel Osteen, and other inspirational speakers. Listening to these gifted pastors and speakers really excites me and puts a smile in my heart, which in turn puts a smile on my face. I know I'm more "beautiful" after a session with one of them. For intellectual stimulation and pure relaxation, I watch *Jeopardy* and *Wheel of Fortune*.

Whenever I feel mentally low, besides turning to God, music uplifts me. It has always been an important part of my life. I discovered at an early age that music has a great effect on my mental state. I could enter into another world through the soothing or dramatic sound of classical music. I played the violin in my school orchestra and studied ballet. It was a thrill to attend the Philadelphia symphony orchestra's concerts, even though I could only afford to sit in the "nose-bleed seats" and could barely see the orchestra from that height.

I sang in school choruses and in the choir at Salem Baptist Church, although I still don't have that gospel sound. Through the years, I've come to appreciate most kinds of music, favoring jazz, classical, gospel, pop, country, and R&B, depending on my mood. As I write this book, I alternate between listening to Smokie Norful's "Nothing without You," Jim Brickman's "Grace," and a CD of French music that a friend put together for me. When I take a break, I put on the Brooklyn Tabernacle Choir's "Amazed." And to relax, I listen to Shirley Horne's "Here's to Life" or a jazz instrumental CD. Lionel Harris's music is constantly played in my car. It really makes me feel good. But not everyone is uplifted by music. Years ago, when I invited a young man I was dating to attend a symphony performance, he fell asleep. What a jolt he got when the orchestra played the forte part of "The Surprise Symphony!"

Music is so powerful that I believe we must be careful of the words we sing and listen to. What are they saying to and about you? How do they make you feel? What do they encourage you to do? How do they affect your attitude? A young woman once told me that she was considering suicide and stopped when she heard a 5th Dimension song on the radio. I thought she was exaggerating until I heard the same story from several other people through the years. This made me realize the responsibility I have as an entertainer and a proud member of The 5th Dimension

Sammy Davis taught me that as a performer, one's attitude is very important. I'll never forget his advice: "When you're onstage, go for the top of the hill. People pay their money to see a show. They don't care about your family or what's happening in your life. Give them your best. They've paid for it." He was so right. Like many other performers, I've gone on stage several times not feeling my best physically, but I've always "gone for the top of the hill." After I had hip surgery, I couldn't walk too well, let alone dance. But I decided my fans deserved the best, so as I mentioned in the last chapter, I had a fantastic bling cane made so I could still perform and have some fun with my temporary prop. The fans all loved it and they lifted my spirits. The same should apply in everyday life, even if you're not a performer. Give everyone around you your best. I guarantee you'll see the results.

Reading positive books is a good way to improve your mood. Besides starting my day by reading my Bible and devotional *(Jesus Calling)*, when time permits, I enjoy reading inspirational books and biographies. Og Mandino is one of my favorite authors. In fact, some years ago I wrote him a fan letter. He not only answered, but he sent me five autographed bookplates. As you can imagine, I treasure them. When I read that Og Mandino died, I felt that I had lost a friend. What kind of books help you to relax or stimulate you mentally? What inspires you? Find something you can always turn to for a positive perspective.

You Don't Have to Grow Old; Grow Bold Instead!

We live in an extremely ageist culture. A gerontologist, psychiatrist, and Pulitzer Prize-winning author named Robert N. Butler first used the term *ageist* back in 1968, a year after Congress passed the Age Discrimination in Employment Act. Despite this act, ageism is alive and well and is constantly reinforced by our youth-obsessed society, which is reflected by Hollywood and the advertising industry. Whereas older people used to be revered and respected, now they're ignored and rejected. But we don't have to buy into that. The baby boomer generation is beginning to change attitudes by being much more proactive in their rejection of stereotypes. We should feel good about ourselves. We should celebrate our looks, our minds, and our years of experience that have given us wisdom and enriched our lives and those of others. Attitude is very important as we mature. Aging is an opportunity to be embraced, a privilege not granted to everybody. Life is a beautiful journey of discovery, fulfillment, and self-evolution. Getting older means feeling confident in your choices. There's pretty much nothing we haven't seen or dealt with sometime during our lives. We *know* we can make this work because we have so much experience to draw on.

Here are a few tips to help you fight ageism by changing your attitude. After all, getting old doesn't happen suddenly; it's a gradual process so let's prepare for it:

1. Stay active, mentally, and physically. Be aware of what's going on in the world.
2. Live in the present and the future, not in the past. Yes, we all have a wealth of experience to draw on and pass on to anyone who wants to listen, but be aware of what's going on now.
3. Listen to today's music. You might not like it all, but you might be surprised that you may like some of it!

4. Learn about social media. You don't have to be on Facebook all day, but at least be aware of what it is and how it works. Your grandchildren will be impressed!

5. Keep in touch with younger people, no matter what your age (or theirs). You'll learn a lot from them, and it will stop you from getting too set in your ways or in your opinions. Younger people see things from a different angle. Find out why they have the opinions they do.

6. If you're single, never give up on love. It can happen anytime, anywhere.

7. Say yes instead of no. Sometimes new experiences can be daunting, but embrace the novelty; don't reject it.

8. Don't count the years. That's guaranteed to make you feel old.

9. If you're feeling creaky and down in the dumps, put on some music and dance.

10. Do something new each day. If not now, when?

11. Don't dwell on your failures. They're part of life. If something doesn't work, find an alternative.

12. Instead of a New Year's resolution, make a New You resolution. You can do that anytime, and give yourself some realistic goals.

13. Stay spiritually alive.

To summarize this chapter on attitude, I encourage you to think beautiful thoughts, and thank God for your many blessings. Start each day with a positive attitude. If you feel good about yourself and your life, it will change the perception of others toward you. By adapting and embracing aging, we make it a positive choice, instead of trying to remain unrealistically youthful.

And while you're at it, clean your emotional house! We all cling to old grievances and outdated opinions. If you don't think you have any clutter, ask a friend you can trust. One who truly loves you and will tell you the truth. But be ready for an attitude adjustment, if necessary.

Bottom line: *be you!* God made each of us special in our own unique way. We are all a garden of beautiful flowers. (Just don't display your thorns!) Keep your mind healthy, kind, and loving to all.

Chapter 3

CONFIDENCE

My after-forty face felt far more comfortable than anything I
lived with previously. Self-confidence was a powerful beauty
potion; I looked better because I felt better. Failure and grief
as well as success and love had served me well. Finally, I was
tapping into that most hard won of youth dews—wisdom.

—Nancy Collins

I wasn't a confident child. I was very shy because I was different: a little
Black girl raised in a White world. Fortunately, my mother taught me
self-assurance. She told me that if I worked hard and believed in God,
I could become anything I wanted. That gave me such a strong foundation
and belief in myself. And it was because of her I was able to become the
Florence LaRue you see before you. I always tried to excel in sports, music,
and dancing. In fact, I wanted to do the best I possibly could in anything I
set out to do. That's what gave me the confidence I eventually developed,
to feel I belonged, because I believed I was as good as anyone else.

So many people don't have relationships with fathers, but those who
do, often seem to have more confidence. My parents divorced when I was
quite young so I didn't have a father in my life. I was always looking for
Daddy. I'm sure a lot of women will relate to that.

As parents, we have a responsibility to encourage our children to be
confident. We have to show them the way. Don't try to make your children
into what you are or what you want them to be. Discover their abilities and
encourage them to be themselves and the best boys or girls they can be.

Try to encourage them not to compare themselves with others, and have them urge their friends to be better, root for those who are better, not try to compete, and find their own talent. On the other hand, there are schools where everyone gets to play and nobody wins. That's not good either. We have to be realistic in a loving way.

When I first joined The 5th Dimension, I was intimidated. Even though I had sung in school and church, my training was in dance and violin. I studied ballet and interpretive dancing as a youth. I was also self-conscious because I couldn't riff like most of the Black vocalists of that era. As a matter of fact, The 5th Dimension was accused by a few people of trying to sound White because we didn't sound like the Black recording artists whose music was being played on the radio. Sometimes, you just can't win!

But the Lord showed me that just as there is only one original Aretha Franklin, there is only one original Florence LaRue, and I should use my God-given talents to the best of my ability and not try to be a carbon copy of anyone else. It took me a while and some trial and error before I was able to accept this fact. My aha moment occurred when I was asked to sing the lead to the song "I'm Going Home" in The 5th Dimension show. I tried to copy the runs of Philippe of the Spinners, whose recorded version of the song I really liked. Needless to say, I was horrible. Then one day I heard Johnny Mathis on the radio singing the same song, without Philippe's riffs, and it sounded great. Johnny had sung in his style without trying to be a carbon copy of Philippe. I actually took the song out of the show because I found one that suited my vocal style much better.

I'm most confident when I'm on stage if I know the material. I become Ms. LaRue, my alter ego. I'm secure in the knowledge that I am a good performer. I realize where my gift lies. I still continue to take vocal lessons. I'm not confident when I'm not prepared. If you're well prepared, for anything in life, you're more likely to be confident. That's a lesson I've learned and apply to everything I do. I can't stress enough that preparation really is the good foundation for confidence. Whatever I did, whether it was teaching, performing, or taking part in marathons, I have always made sure I knew what I was doing and had planned ahead. When I was in beauty pageants, I was confident—not because I was the most beautiful but I was always prepared. I was taught how to walk and how to behave in front of the judges, and I had carefully rehearsed my talent piece. I wanted to win, but that wasn't my main objective. What I really wanted was to be discovered and be in the movies. I won a talent competition and was asked to join a singing group.

I'm nearsighted, so for a good part of my earlier career, I couldn't see the audience. That was worked well for me because I was very shy, so I could almost forget they were there. Then I started wearing contact lenses. Surprisingly, I actually preferred being able to see everyone. Instead of finding it intimidating, my shyness gradually disappeared because I enjoyed communicating with the audience. When I sing, I'm conversing with them through the song, and being able to see those faces helped. I've seen men cry when I sing a sad song. That's so fulfilling, because I want my audience to feel something. That means I've connected. There's a fine line between arrogance and confidence, and we always have to be careful about that. I like to have a little tension before I get on stage. It's a kind of thrill, an anticipation of visiting with my friends: the audience. That gives me the adrenalin surge. A lot is talked about stage fright, but it isn't really "fright." It's more about ego, because what you're saying to yourself is "I hope they like me" rather than "Let me entertain them."

Two of the most self-assured performers I ever met were Frank Sinatra and Sammy Davis. Another is Johnny Mathis. He's extraordinarily humble. He shows his confidence in a different way, by sharing his talent with others.

Your attitude is so very important to your beauty. What you think about you really affects what others think about you. Are you confident with your appearance? Do you check your attitude?

Think about it. How many people have you ever heard say they were satisfied with their appearance? Most people complain about their weight, their hair (too curly or too straight) their height, or some other physical characteristic that they are unhappy with. Few people point out their good features or thank God for their good physical and mental health. I know I am happier when I just try to be the best Florence I can be—mentally, physically, and spiritually. Healthy and happy. There is no other person like me or like you.

Trying to be someone you're not just doesn't work. Instead, if you aspire to be the best version of yourself, you'll be much happier and more confident. In order to be truly confident (not arrogant), you have to be comfortable in your skin. Most of us don't take time to get to know ourselves and to love ourselves. It's hard to say I love me because it sounds arrogant, but we should all feel good about ourselves. I've seen overweight women with beautiful hair, but they focus on the weight. And people who aren't what society considers beautiful can nevertheless be striking. If you're intelligent, kind, and generous of spirit, then you are beautiful. You're letting your inner light shine.

As I said before, constantly strive to be the best version of yourself. Don't compare yourself to others, either physically or mentally. Bottom line: *be you.* God made each of us special in our own way: a garden of beautiful flowers. (Just don't display any thorns!) Your attitude is so very important to your beauty. I don't want to seem like a religious nut, but I truly believe that God made us all special and we all have talents. So we need to be confident, knowing that God didn't make any mistake. A good spiritual foundation also helps to build our confidence.

Another important thing to bear in mind is that it's alright to make mistakes. Failure isn't final. Failure is a stop on the journey, not a destination. And the great thing about mistakes is that we can learn from them. I feel like society doesn't give us enough room to fail and to correct our mistakes. So much emphasis is put on the negative and the news headlines are frequently negative. The deadlier, the more widely catastrophic the event, the more attention is given to it.

Remember, perfection doesn't exist. Some of us performers in the magazines or on TV shows may not look the same without our vast team of stylists, makeup artists, etc. Some of us may even wear two pairs of Spanx, crippling shoes, layers of makeup, false lashes, and heaven knows what else. (I even had an eyelash come off on stage once.)

So here are some tips to help you feel confident about who you are and how you look and to show you the way to let your inner light shine. I don't suggest you do all of them all the time, but gradually try to incorporate some of these principals into your daily life.

- Don't buy into the myth of stereotypes—how we *should* look or behave at this point in our lives. We all have very different life experiences, which have included joy, tragedy, disappointment, success, failure, etc. And those experiences have all shaped us and made us different from each other. Be proud of that difference; embrace those experiences.

- Give yourself positive reinforcement. Tell yourself you're beautiful, kind, happy—whatever makes you feel good. Compliment yourself, whether it's to tell yourself you look great or that you've done a good job.
- Compliment other people. Boosting someone else's confidence will boost yours too.
- Silence your inner critic. If that little voice inside you starts whispering that you're not good enough, tell it to go away.
- Don't compare yourself to others. There will always be someone younger, prettier, richer, cleverer, more successful, etc. Celebrate your own triumphs; don't envy someone else's. Besides which, you never know how they really feel inside or what challenges they're facing. Chances are your life is just as good, if not better.
- Keep reminding yourself about all the ways in which your life is special.
- If you're not feeling confident, no one needs to know. Fake it! If you pretend to be self-assured for long enough, it will become a habit. Hey, presto! You're confident!
- Surround yourself with positive people. Positivity is infectious.
- Dress well, and groom yourself. Clean hair, fresh clothes, and a little makeup can transform your mood. Even if you're going to the market, look good. It will boost your self-image.
- Be prepared. Whatever task you have to tackle, prepare well in advance. Knowing you have everything in order will boost your confidence to no end.
- Remember your posture. Sit and stand tall. Slouching is sloppy; good posture looks confident.
- List your best qualities. And enlist your friends! Ask someone you truly trust to tell you about yourself and how you can improve yourself. I once asked this of four people and they all said the same positive things, but one said something I could improve upon. I was really grateful for that input. I thanked her for that because her comments are helping me to change. I'm working on

it. Interestingly, the suggestion didn't hurt my feelings because deep within in me, I knew it was true. Now that's a real friend.

- Reassess your self-image. Stop constantly reminding yourself you have to lose a few pounds, you have new lines on your forehead, or you're not good enough. Replace a bad self-image with good self-confidence. Think about why you keep seeing you in such a negative way, and change your attitude toward yourself!

- Think positive, not negative. Don't think about what you can't do. Focus on what you can do.

- Set small achievable goals instead of aiming for the stars on day one. For example, if you want to lose twenty pounds, set five-pound goals. Choose an event—a birthday, a wedding, or a special outing—and determine to lose five pounds by then. Then set another five-pound goal.

- Focus on solutions rather than problems. For instance, if you're always late for work, ask yourself why and work out a plan to prevent that from happening.

- Tackle something on your to-do list. You'll feel so self-satisfied when you can cross it off!

- Tidy your desk or work area. You'll feel much more organized and in control.

- If you're dealing with a problem and you're not sure how to tackle it, think of someone you admire and imagine how he or she would deal with it.

Quick Confidence Boosters

If you're having a down moment and need a quick shot in the arm to boost your confidence, try doing one or more of the following:

- Smile. You'll look and feel better. Smiling is the cheapest cosmetic!
- Listen to a high-power song that gives you positive energy.
- Think of three people who are important to you—who you love and who love you back.
- Be grateful. Think of all the blessings that have happened in your life. It can be something as simple as remembering a thoughtful birthday gift someone gave you.

- Dance to a favorite song. It's guaranteed to make you feel better.
- Go out into nature for a few minutes.
- Take a quick shower and sprinkle some peppermint oil onto the shower floor so the scent surrounds you. You'll feel refreshed and ready to tackle the rest of the day.

So now that I've encouraged you to be confident, let me tell you about the time I took it just a little too far!

I once attended an elegant affair while knowing that I was looking my best—flawless makeup, fabulous hair, and dressed to the nines. My confidence was through the roof! As I took the long walk from the ladies' room to my seat, all eyes, male and female, were on me. The more they looked, the higher in the air my nose rose. When I arrived at my seat, I discovered that I had toilet paper stuck in the top of my panty hose, which caused my dress to be raised and I was totally exposed! What a way to learn the difference between confidence and arrogance. Had I been humbler, I'm sure someone would have told me of my predicament, and my embarrassment would have been lessened.

Chapter 4

STYLE ICONS

A s I mentioned in the previous chapter, your attitude is so very important to your beauty, and perfection doesn't exist. However, cultivating and creating a signature style that is perfect for you is key to growing and maintaining a storehouse of confidence. Having a style that others associate with your best self is powerful in bringing you confidence while being inspiring to others. Now this takes time, patience, and maybe a little help from your friends. So while you're trying out a few of my tips to help you feel confident about who you are, find two or three individuals—celebrities or not—whose style you find appealing and creative—maybe whose look most closely resembles your ideal version of yourself or at least has many of its elements.

It also helps if she has a similar body type as you because if she's a true icon, she's already figured out how to look her best and accentuate the positive! This person doesn't have to be a celebrity. He or she can be a friend or acquaintance you admire.

Nowadays, it seems that there is a plethora of beautiful young women both in the public eye and just living in the neighborhoods. Where did they all come from? Interestingly, the image of what is beautiful has really *crossed over*. Afro American girls are sporting blonde hair, and the Caucasian girls are wearing braids. I love that. When I was a kid, it was hard to find anyone who even remotely resembled the way I looked. Early on, I tried to copy mostly White hairstyles and makeup because they were the only models in the magazines that were available. During the course of my career, I have been privileged to work with some really talented designers and makeup artists, both Black and White.

Growing up in Glenside, Pennsylvania, was very challenging for me. So challenging, in fact, that I have unconsciously erased much of it from my memory. I do have vivid memory impressions of feeling that I did not fit in and being lonely much of the time. You see, geography forced me to live in a peculiar place—on the line that divided the Black and White population and the school district. As a result, I attended schools populated almost entirely by White students for all but one of my school years. Neither race fully accepted me. The Black people felt that my family thought we were better than they were and that we "acted White." And there was an unspoken prejudice from many of the Whites—more from the parents than the children.

Needless to say, that greatly distorted my ideas about what was beautiful. I remember feeling very embarrassed when the book *The Story of Little Black Sambo* was read in my elementary school class. Everyone was laughing and all eyes turned to me, the only Black face in the room.

The only Afro American people I saw on television when I was a child were Amos and Andy. I didn't have *Jet* or *Ebony* magazines to show me positive images of Black women with whom I could identify. I grew up with the impression that used to be so prevalent in the Black community: that a beautiful Afro American woman was one who was light skinned and slim and had "good" (straight!) hair.

When I was about ten years old, my mother took me to see Lena Horne at Carnegie Hall. I can still remember how beautiful I thought she was. It was actually then that I decided that I wanted to be in show business. Even at that tender age, I knew that there was something special about Ms. Horne. Now I know that I was impressed not only by the fact that she was a beautiful Black woman but I could sense what I now know was her poise and class. Years later, I would subconsciously use this valuable information to win beauty contests over young ladies who were much prettier than I.

When I became an adult, I used to scrutinize Ms. Horne's photos. I studied how her makeup was applied and how she dressed. I felt I couldn't be as beautiful as she was, but I wanted to learn about and absorb her elegance. Looking back, I realize she was my first style icon.

What made her so special? First of all, she was the epitome of glamour. Like all style icons, she knew how to accentuate her best features, especially her lovely shoulders, long legs, and tiny waist. She almost always wore form-fitting, off-the-shoulder gowns, which showed off her assets perfectly. Ms. Horne always looked classy and elegant. She dressed like a celebrity performer but never overdid the bling. Her hair, makeup, and accessories were subtle, so the beautiful clothes she wore spoke for themselves, reinforcing her star quality.

She was also extremely intelligent and a principled civil rights activist, which added to her charisma. Beauty *and* brains are a heady combination. She was a lot more than a pretty face, which made her a role model for many young women of my generation.

Many years later, I had the privilege of meeting her in person, but I was so in awe of her beauty I didn't know what to say or do. She was very kind and gracious to my mother and me and posed for a photo after her show.

When it comes to beauty influences, Sophia Loren is another woman at the top of my list. I was always fascinated by her signature eye makeup, which of course, emphasized her extraordinary eyes. Even though she had a voluptuous, hourglass figure, she always appeared classy (but still very sexy). She favored classic clothes that were always beautifully cut to emphasize her curves.

I sat behind Ms. Loren at Frank Sinatra's funeral and was impressed with her natural beauty. She wore little makeup and had her hair pulled back in a chignon yet was still one of the most glamorous women present.

I was fortunate enough to meet both of my early style icons in the flesh, and neither of them disappointed. I believe it was because they weren't just about beauty and clothes. They both exuded confidence and carried themselves with great dignity, seemingly oblivious to the impact they had on everyone around them.

I've drawn up a list of style icons, both present day and from the past, and given a little analysis of just why each one stands apart from the crowd of celebrities and fashionistas. I've also chosen women with very different body shapes so you can see how they use style and fashion to exploit their assets.

- Iman

  The Somali fashion model, actress, and entrepreneur was the first Black supermodel to hit the runway. She's truly in a class of her own. While there are many beautiful Black women, Iman has her own very distinct style. I had the opportunity to meet her in person also. She was very gracious, with an inner beauty that radiated from her. Standing five feet, nine inches, and weighing around 115 pounds, she has a stunning, willowy figure that can wear just about anything she chooses but now tends to gravitate toward classically elegant clothes.

- Audrey Hepburn

Audrey Hepburn is, without a doubt, an official classic style icon. Her fashion staples are still in the closets of most well-dressed women today, even though they probably don't realize it. The slim-fitted pants, the little black dress, the crisp white shirt, flat ballet pumps, and understated, chic accessories are all courtesy of the delightful Ms. Hepburn. But the secret of her style was not just about her looks. It had a lot to do with the confident, carefree way she wore her clothes.

- Michelle Obama

Oh, those fabulous arms! Study her look, but do remember if your arms aren't like hers, cover them up! She is very adventurous, and her outfits don't always work, but I love that she's prepared to make mistakes. However, most of the time, she hits it out of the ballpark.

Mrs. Obama has a very different body type from the previous style icons I've listed.

She's five feet, eleven, and is beautifully toned and shapely. She embraces and celebrates her size with dramatic colors and flamboyant jewelry.

When she became first lady, she was very aware that she had to adhere to certain guidelines, which couldn't have been easy for such a fiercely independent lady. And as our first Black first lady, she knew she would be in for some particularly harsh criticism if she overstepped any boundaries. I think she did a fantastic job, especially as she made a point of celebrating young American designers.

It's been interesting to see how her style has altered since she left the White House; her choices are significantly edgier. But even though her style may have changed, I predict her status as a fashion icon will remain for many years to come.

By the way, I met her, and she looked as good in person as she does in her photos.

- Jackie Kennedy

Speaking of first ladies, how can I possibly exclude her? She's probably one of the greatest style icons of all time. She mesmerized the public (both in the US and internationally) with her chic yet simple fashion sense. As our youngest first lady, she knew she had to conform to previous norms but was determined to put her own stamp on the look. Mrs. Kennedy successfully transformed conservative clothes into headline-making fashion statements, leaving a legacy we still celebrate today.

- Sarah Jessica Parker

At five feet, three, this successful actress, producer, and designer certainly has her own signature style. She has great fun with her looks and injects her personality into every outfit. SJP dresses so well for her body type—small but very athletic. Like Mrs. Obama, she likes to display her toned arms and shoulders. She wears very daring clothes that might be too much for some of us, but that doesn't stop us looking and learning. We don't have to go all the way with her unique statement pieces, but we can pick one or two elements from her total look and adapt them for our more modest lifestyles. For example, she'll pair a masculine leather jacket with a superfeminine floaty dress and often choose unusual color combinations and somehow make them work. And of course, as we know from her role in *Sex in the City,* her shoes are always worth a second look!

- Diane Keaton

  Since her break out role in *Annie Hall,* Diane Keaton has always been one to watch style-wise and is a good example of aging gracefully without losing her own signature quirky quality. The slacks, waistcoat, white shirt, and tie look that she introduced us to in *Annie Hall* still looks great on her, and she often wears some version of that even now, although her look has evolved over the decades. She accessorizes with hats and interesting glasses, while her favorite color palette is black and white. I also love that she'll challenge red-carpet expectations by wearing a beautifully tailored tuxedo instead of an elaborate evening gown.

- Meryl Streep

  She famously said she "couldn't care less" about fashion, so I suppose she's an accidental style icon. At five feet, six, and a little fuller figured than she once was, she never fails to impress. She knows absolutely what works for her body and never tries to be something she isn't. Her red-carpet fashion choices are always spot-on. Ms. Streep never wears anything too tight or too low-cut, and sticks with a neutral color palette, which perfectly suits her pale complexion and blonde hair. She knows her shoulders are her best asset and often shows them off. Her clothes are simple and elegant, and she often enhances her outfits with one gorgeous accessory, like a statement belt or a dramatic pair of earrings. She really is a star on and off the big screen.

- Helen Mirren

  A curvy five-foot, four-inch lady, the ageless Helen Mirren has evolved from a sexy young siren into a grande dame of the theater. And her style has changed to match her status. Like Meryl Streep, her clothes are figure hugging but never too tight. She owns the red carpet wherever she goes and knows exactly what to show and what to hide. I think the most attractive element is that she always seems to be having fun with her looks and never plays it safe. She wears bright colors, bold accessories, and towering heels and never takes the safe option. Ultimately, she always manages to look effortlessly gorgeous and still oozes sex appeal. Ms. Mirren also has a lot of fun with her beautiful silver fox hair, sometimes tinting it to match her gown. Awesome!

- Angela Bassett

The stunning Ms. Bassett is gorgeous! She's in great shape and loves to display her toned arms. As she explains, "I believe we all have something—great legs, beautiful hair—so find your something, be proud of it, and accentuate it."

- Ashley Graham

The stunning model and activist Ashley Graham is an inspirational style icon for curvy ladies. She rejects the phrase *plus-size*. As she says, "Plus-size? More like my size." And that just about sums it up—*her* size, *her* style. No old-fashioned rules, no hiding under tent dresses, no sticking with safe colors. She's big, bold, and brave—and that's what she projects in every outfit she wears. Ashley shows her lingerie (and her hourglass figure) beneath sheer tops, wears her skirts above her knees, rocks crop tops, wears white on white, and happily flaunts her ample cleavage. She'll sport a skintight outfit one day, and the next, she'll step out in a stunning pair of baggy pants with a clingy top. But the secret to her success as a style icon isn't just her choice of clothes. She's always perfectly groomed and exudes confidence and positive energy. While many women may not feel comfortable imitating some of her more adventurous choices, we can all learn a lot from her attitude. As she says, "It's not just about our size. It's about our mind, our heart, our emotions. We get so wrapped up in this size conversation."

That's my personal list of influencers and role models. So have some fun finding your own personal style icon. You'll soon find yourself incorporating her flair into what you wear!

Chapter 5

STYLE

So many women just don't know how great they really are.
They come to us all vogue outside and vague on the inside.

—Mary Kay Ash

As an only child for the first ten years of my life, I always had new clothes, even though my mother didn't have a lot of money. I usually wore very feminine dresses with matching hats and gloves. My wardrobe was divided into "Sunday clothes," "school clothes," and "playclothes." For school and play, I had to wear black-and-white or brown-and-white Buster Brown oxfords. I was always anxious for Sunday to arrive so I could wear my shiny black Mary Jane shoes in the winter or my white Mary Janes in the summer. My mother used to say that I had champagne taste and beer money because, without knowing the price, I would always choose the most expensive item of clothing or shoes. And I still do.

Years later, when I returned to my high school to be inducted into the hall of fame, I had the opportunity to talk to the gentleman who was the custodian when I attended the school. He told me that I always wore my hair and clothes differently from the other girls. I don't remember this, but I can imagine it being true because I do enjoy being different. If I attend a formal affair where I know most of the women will be wearing scanty beaded gowns, I'll wear a very classic, simple, unbeaded gown! That's *my* style.

So what is style, and how do we become stylish? My favorite definition of style is from Iris Apfel, the ninetysomething-year-old New York fashion icon. She said, "The key to style is learning who you are, which takes years. There's no how-to road map to style. It's about self-expression and, above all, attitude." That is absolutely true. But I do believe there are some pointers that will help you develop your own particular style or perhaps rediscover your style, which might have gotten lost over the years.

The first thing to remember is this: fashion is ageist, but style is ageless. I believe that mature women can be stylish without being slavish. We're living in the best time to be able to stay true to ourselves, style-wise. There are very few dos and don'ts and some maybes. After all, what on earth does age appropriate even mean?

There's no doubt that as we get older, styling can become more challenging. We create our own rigid rules about what we can and can't wear, becoming our own worst critics. Having said that, there are some things that should be avoided. Those of us who embraced miniskirts, towering heels, bare midriffs, and psychedelic colors probably agree that while we looked great at the time, we should definitely abandon some of those concepts now. Don't get me wrong. I'm not saying we shouldn't look glamorous (and sexy when appropriate!), but we do need to accept there are some limitations. For example, no matter how great your legs are, I don't think our second act knees and upper thighs benefit from seeing too much daylight! A little cleavage is great, but it's definitely time to put aside anything too plunging and retain a little more mystery. Remember those adorable, skimpy little tops we used to wear without a bra underneath? They're a definite no-no.

Having listed a few items that we need to firmly relegate to our own personal history books and photo albums, what does that leave us with? In my view, a whole lot of fantastic choices.

Choose Your Role Model

The secret of good style is to tailor your look to fit your body type, size, age, and personality. Our favorite style icons (which I discussed in a previous chapter) all have one thing in common: they know their bodies and what suits them best. They long ago decided on the most flattering colors for their complexions and the best cuts for their body types. That's why they're style icons. When I was a young woman, my particular role models were Lena Horne and Audrey Hepburn, and now I've added Helen Mirren, Jane Fonda, Angela Bassett, and Michelle Obama. These women are all built differently. They don't wear the same style of clothes, yet they all look sensational. If you study photos of them all, you'll see none of them really deviate from the core look they have chosen for themselves.

So the first thing to do is take a look at your body shape. Don't be overly critical. (I know that's difficult.) Then try to find the style icon that most closely represents your shape and preferred style. That will give you a starting point. Take a look at what they wear and how they wear it. Michelle Obama, for instance, likes big, bold patterns and bright colors, while Helen Mirren and Meryl Streep make far more classic choices. You can pick up so many little tips just by seeing what your favorite icon is wearing. It doesn't mean you have to replicate her outfits; just learn those tricks! If there isn't anyone famous you admire, check out Pinterest, which has lots of examples of different looks.

Once you've identified your role model and studied her, it's time to develop your own style. Mine is either all out flamboyant or simply elegant. Sometimes you want to have fun and put on all the bells and whistles, and that's great if you're comfortable with this. Equally, simple and elegant always works.

Be Objective

I gradually learned what colors looked good on me and what styles to wear. I also let my mirror be my guide, and I'm brutally honest with myself. Don't try to convince yourself you look good in something just because it was expensive, because you love the color, or because it looked good on someone else!

If you're going somewhere special, try the entire outfit on in advance, take a photo, and see how it looks. That will give you plenty of time to make any tweaks or changes before the big event. Also, when you try on a dress or top, move in it. I learned that lesson the hard way! I wore a beautiful strapless gown for a 5th Dimension photo shoot that fit perfectly (or so I thought). When I saw the photo, I realized that when I stood up straight, the dress slipped a bit, exposing more of me than I desired! And to make matters worse, I didn't discover this in time to contact the photographer so he could change the photo before it was duplicated. If I had only thought to try it all out earlier, I would have saved myself a great deal of embarrassment.

Shopping for New Items

You don't have to spend a lot of money to look good. Don't be frightened to experiment and accessorize. I often purchase inexpensive clothes then substitute more expensive, interesting buttons. It's such a great way to transform a simple outfit into something more stylish and individual. These buttons can cost $5 a piece or more, but it is worth the investment. Even expensive dresses and jackets can have cheap buttons or buttons of the wrong color! I once had a lovely red blouse that had rather cheap white buttons. I swapped them for vintage red buttons, transforming the blouse into a stunning piece. But why stop at buttons? If you see an item with unrealized potential, grab it! I once found a beautiful wool dress that was marked $25 (down from over $200). That was a bargain in itself, but I convinced the saleslady to sell it for $20 because the belt was missing. I ended up spending $100 on a stunning belt to wear with it. Now that might seem like a real extravagance, but let me assure you I have worn that belt more times than I can count with lots of other outfits, and I still wear that $20 dress more than ten years later. I believe you have to be wise with your spending.

Take time to rummage around in vintage and secondhand stores. You just never know what you're going to find when you walk in. They're like an Aladdin's cave with untold treasures. You just have to be patient.

Try on different designers' clothes and see which complement you. My favorite designers are Chanel, Armani, and St. John because of their classic designs, quality materials, and attention to details. Because they are quite pricy, I always purchase them on sale. But remember it isn't necessary to wear designer clothes to be beautiful or stylish. I have in my closet some lovely pieces from Target, Walmart, TJ Maxx, and Marshalls.

Speaking of bargains, some of the best bargains turn out to be the costliest mistakes. We've all reached the "been there, done that" stage, so let's make sure we don't fall in love with a high-maintenance piece; check the washing and cleaning directions before you buy. It's very annoying to buy a perfect top to take on vacation, thinking it can be washed and hung up to dry, only to find it's a dry-clean-only piece.

When you go shopping, make a list—not just of what you want to buy but of the favorite pieces you already have and love so when you spot something that will work nicely, it's a no-brainer.

And remember that just because you wear a particular size in one designer's line, it doesn't mean that you will wear the same size in all lines. Designers tend to cut differently. Curvy ladies, like I, may wear different sizes in tops and bottoms. Don't be a slave to a number. Buy what fits. Remember nobody is going to see the label! I find that many dresses are too small in the bust, so I purchase the larger size and have the bottom altered.

Second Act Style Tips

Chic women never bow to the trends. They keep an arsenal of classic pieces that always flatter and work, despite the season or latest craze. We Americans would do well to learn from French women. While we fill our closets with lots of random items, they purchase a few well-made classic items each season. If you're wearing an outfit in a color that flatters you, in a style that flatters you and that is tailored for your body, you will ooze confidence.

Be careful when wearing T-shirts with writing on them. I once had a beautiful blue T-shirt that had "I'm Blessed" written across the chest. I was wearing it one day when a man read it and said, "You sure are!"

We all have parts of our figure that we don't like, whether we are size 2, 12, or 20. I've never met a woman who honestly loves everything about her figure. Instead, celebrate your shape. If you've got great legs, let them be seen; if you have narrow hips, emphasize them. Concentrate on your assets. Your less attractive bits will fade into insignificance.

What you're wearing should make a statement. So ask yourself, "What statement am I making?" I remember I once walked into a room dressed up to the nines. Someone came up to me and said, "I don't know who you are, but you must be somebody."

Anchor your look with one expensive-looking piece. Some women can make the simplest outfit look impossibly chic. How do they do it? It has a lot to do with the fit, of course, but there's another subtle way these ladies are elevating their outfit. It might be a great leather belt, a special pair of earrings, or a statement purse, but in every case, one expensive-looking accessory adds infinitely more polish.

Know what to conceal and what to reveal. Too much cleavage can be too much! Deep, plunging, cleavage-flashing tops are not a good idea for a stylish second acter! Instead, try a boatneck cut. It's so much more flattering and sexier, and as an added bonus, it has an elongating effect on the neck. A good rule of thumb is to play up places you dab perfume, like your wrists, forearms, and collar. And be careful about the length of your skirts and dresses. Too short just doesn't look good, and too long can be very aging.

Nothing beats great tailoring. I learned that from The 5th Dimension's first designer, Boyd Clopton. I really learned about fit from him. I have to have almost everything altered, and it's definitely worth the trouble. Well-fitting clothes always look good. The difference between sophisticated and sloppy is all about the fit. Choose items with some structure over loose-fitting or baggy styles.

Before you leave the house, check yourself in a full-length mirror. And if you don't have one, that should be your first investment!

And keep it simple. Bling can be fun, prints can be fun, but be careful how you put them together.

Plan Ahead

Do some advance planning. Instead of rushing in the morning and grabbing the first thing that comes to hand, lay out your clothes the night before or even plan for the whole week. It will save you a great deal of time, and you'll never have the frustration of finding there's a button missing or a stain on your shirt just as you're leaving the house. It also avoids suffering from outfit regret. (You know that moment when you realize you just don't look right but don't have time to change.) It's not magic—or rocket science. The pulled-together women you see out and about really *did* try to look that way. A little advance planning will guarantee your look is more put together than thrown together. I also start packing my suitcase a week before I travel so I can coordinate outfits and make sure everything is in proper wearing condition.

Give yourself plenty of time to get ready, especially for an important date. This goes hand in hand with readying your outfit at bedtime. Not only will it save you from running out of the house with a button missing or scruffy shoes, but it'll also give you a few extra minutes to add a belt or a special piece of jewelry to polish off the look.

Comfort Zone

I know I've emphasized how important it is to know your style and stick to it, but remember we girls still love to have fun! So while you're in the mall doing some retail therapy for good classic items, step outside of your comfort zone before you step into the fitting room. Try on a color you've never worn before or a different cut of jeans. You might surprise yourself. And if it doesn't work, don't buy it!

Underwear

Don't get me started on undergarments! How many times have you seen a woman's beautiful dress or top spoiled by bra straps showing or a flowing dress ruined by being able to see her underwear?

Stylish women know the foundation of a great look is good underwear. Plan for the fabric and silhouette of your look with the *right bra*, panties, and shapewear to provide the support you need, whether it's to ensure you're not inadvertently giving your office a peep show when you forget your slip or preventing a nip slip on date night.

The right underwear makes your clothes fit and look their best! And remember, ladies, if your "girls" are sagging, it can add ten years to your age. Be fitted for the correct bra size. You'd be amazed how many women have never actually consulted an expert to find out what their size really is. One recent studied showed 80 percent of women are wearing incorrectly fitting bras. Babies, menopause, exercise, and weight losses and gains all change our bra sizes, yet more often than not, we continue to buy the same size. Most department stores will fit you for free, and there's a good chance you'll find you've been wearing the wrong size for years.

And most women should have one pair of shapewear. No matter how skinny you are, there's always one outfit that may show a bulge you'd prefer to hide!

To Wear or Not to Wear

- Dress for the occasion. The well-dressed women in the room are always the ones who got the dress code memo. They look polished and appropriate. They're never trying to pull down the hem of their miniskirts in a room full of more conservative looks. When in doubt, err on the side of being dressier. There's nothing worse than feeling underdressed and dowdy while everyone else is glammed up.

- Dress for the weather. It sounds simple enough, but dressing sensibly goes a long way in the style department. Check the weather before you leave the house to avoid being that girl trudging through the snow in her flats or dodging puddles in your wide-leg flares. When traveling from warm weather to cold, layering is best. Purchase a lightweight, packable coat rather than taking a bulky, heavy winter coat.

Giving Clothes a Facelift

I like to remake clothes so I get more wear out of them. For instance, about twenty years ago, I bought a lovely, simple, black jersey gown with long sleeves and a simple neckline. It had a slit on one side and covered buttons from one shoulder to the slit. I wore it in its original design several times, and then I replaced the covered buttons with rhinestone buttons. After wearing the gown this way a few times, I had my dressmaker remove one sleeve and put the original buttons back on the gown. The gown cost me about $200 (remember it was at least twenty years ago), but I still receive compliments when I wear it.

Princess Diana had tremendous style, but with all her fabulous resources, she often remade dresses. One time, she attached the top of one gown to the skirt of another. Of course, she looked sensational. I've done that too and given a new lease of life to a rather dull dress. Be imaginative. Have fun.

Make Your Clothes Last

As you now know, I keep my clothes for years. The reason they last so well is that I take good care of them. Here are a few suggestions that will help you extend the life of your clothes:

- Never lounge in your good clothes. When I'm relaxing at home, I like to wear either a comfortable long skirt with a T-shirt or one of my sweat suits. (I find them more comfortable than jeans.) So when you get home, change into your favorite leggings or sweatpants. There's absolutely no reason why you should be curled up on the sofa, watching TV with your cat, while you're wearing your best clothes.
- Fold and hang up your clothes every night. Your clothes aren't just going to magically unwrinkle after you've tossed them on the floor. Get in the habit of hanging up your clothes (or folding knits) immediately after you take them off to ensure they're ready the next time you want to wear them. Keep an eye out for items that need to go to the cleaners or jeans that might be due for a wash. Sorting them daily means you won't be surprised by spots and stains you can treat immediately. It'll quickly become a habit that will save you so much grief when you're getting dressed in a hurry.
- Always keep a fashion emergency kit handy. We can prepare all we want to, but accidents happen to us all. Keep an emergency kit with a purse-size instant-stain remover, safety pins, Band-Aids, and double-sided tape handy, and you'll be ready when blisters, a broken zipper, or a snagged hemline strikes. And remember to pack it when you go away. You'll be so happy you did. I have lots of memories of members of The 5th Dimension coming to me for thread or safety pins.

Color

Embrace color: bright and bold color will jazz up your look and perk up your skin tone. Most of us like black, navy, gray, and white, but accessorize with some bright colors. Experiment with some more unusual shades like turquoise, burnt orange, and salmon for a trendy, sophisticated edge. All these colors pair well with black, white, and navy, which are in your capsule wardrobe. If you're nervous about color initially, just try adding a scarf. If you find you like the new look, then you can invest in an item of clothing in the new hue.

You should know what "your" color is. What colors complement your skin and hair? What makes you feel energetic, sensuous, and confident? I used to wear red so much that if I wasn't wearing red, some people would ask me, "Where's your red?" I have added electric blue and turquoise to my wardrobe because I discovered that those colors are very complementary to my coloring and I feel good when I wear them.

And remember our hair and complexion change over the years, so make sure the colors you're wearing now suit you now.

As a guide, you should consider the following tips:

- Stand in front of a well-lit mirror and hold a piece of white paper beside your face.
- If your skin seems yellow or sallow, it means you have a warm skin tone, so earthy colors are the palette for you. Try burnt orange, terra-cotta, and golden fall colors. They'll look great on you. You could also try apple-green or turquoise, as they work well for warm skin tones too. Sometimes a bright, white shirt can be harsh, so try cream or ivory, which is softer and more flattering.
- A cool skin tone will look pink, rosy, or blueish-red against white paper. So icy-blue, royal-blue, cerise, and blue-greens are the colors you should gravitate toward. Additionally, silver jewelry is a great accessory for this color palette and your skin tone.

Accessories

Accessorize thoughtfully. I always try to wear at least one accessory, whether it's a statement necklace, a snappy purse, or a great pair of earrings. A solid statement piece can take an ensemble from dull to dazzling in seconds.

But be careful. There is a point at which it becomes just too much, and the chicest women know exactly what that point is. Ask yourself if you really need the scarf *and* the statement necklace? Often, the cut of your clothes—an exposed neckline or bare arms—is a great help in determining just what jewelry or accouterments to pair with them. As Coco Chanel famously said, "When accessorizing, always take off the last thing you put on."

Some Final Thoughts on Style

We mature women have to be examples for the younger ones. We won't always get everything right, but it is our responsibility to do our best to set a good example. And we shouldn't be afraid to admit when we've made a mistake or to listen to the young women who have it all together. When I review old 5th Dimension photos, I see that I made my share of mistakes.

Chapter 6

SIMPLIFYING YOUR CLOSET

———∞∞∞———

O nce you've decided on your own personal style, it's time to analyze the contents of your closet. Most of us could benefit from a wardrobe reevaluation. We're all aware that our bodies, faces, and lifestyles have changed over the years, but sometimes our clothes have lagged behind. We cling to those old favorites, which are often past their prime and no longer flatter us.

Now is the time to declutter your closet, create your perfect capsule wardrobe, and simplify dressing so you'll be able to get ready in half the time and look twice as good. First of all, we'll take a look at the essentials you should have in your closet. That will help you to decide what you *shouldn't* have and identify the items you'll probably never wear again. It might help to enlist the help of a friend.

Capsule Wardrobe

Do you have the basics for the perfect "capsule" wardrobe? This is a term coined the 1970s by Susie Faux, a trendsetting boutique owner in London who, appropriately, called her shop Wardrobe. According to Faux, a capsule wardrobe is comprised of some essential items of classic clothing, such as pants, skirts, and jackets, which can then be dressed up or down with seasonal accessories. This idea was then popularized by designer Donna Karan, who in 1985 released a groundbreaking capsule collection of seven interchangeable work-wear pieces.

A capsule wardrobe is the key to being a stylish woman. A few well-chosen items that can be mixed and matched effortlessly make dressing simple, particularly if you're in a hurry. I have several classic black suits with pants and skirts that can go from daytime to evening depending on the jewelry and what is worn under the jacket. I also have several black dresses that are just as versatile.

For me, the perfect capsule wardrobe consists of the following:

1. These days, a nice pair of denim jeans is a staple for both men's and women's wardrobes. Jeans are sold in a variety of styles and colors. If you choose to make them a part of your wardrobe, be sure to choose a style that flatters your particular figure.

2. White jeans or pants are always a glamorous option. Contrary to some old-fashioned concepts, they can be worn summer or winter—in the summer with sandals and a pretty top and in the winter with a sweater and boots. I have several pairs of white pants in different fabrics.

3. A pair of really well-cut pants in a dark, neutral color like black, gray, or navy, depending on your color palette.

4. A crisp, well-fitting white shirt that you can pair with any of your pants or skirts. I have several in different fabrics, some with short and some with long sleeves.

5. A simple little black dress. That was the stylish Audrey Hepburn's go-to outfit. (But remember to knot the belt on the side, never in the front).

6. A black jacket, preferably a smart blazer. This will go with everything from a tank top and jeans to a smart dress.

7. A slim, black skirt. Summer or winter, it's easy to pair with an appropriate top and will take you anywhere from lunch to a business meeting or dinner.

8. Basic tees. Find a make that fits you perfectly, and buy it in as many colors as possible. (But always include black and white or cream). But do be brave. Get at least one in a color that really pops. You won't regret it!

9. Ballet flats. For those of you who, like I, need arch support, you can get low-heeled flats.

10. A pair of dressy heels. I have slingbacks in gold, nude, black, and silver.

If any of these items are missing from your closet, or the ones you have are looking sad or faded or really don't fit anymore (remember you have to be objective!), then it's time to go shopping.

With these core items, you can have some fun individualizing your look, depending on your lifestyle and body shape. For example, once you have your great-fitting jeans, what do you wear with them? If you have narrow hips, bat-winged tops are a good way of showing them off. If your hips are wider, wear patterned and lighter-colored tops. If you're curvy, wear nipped-in tops that draw attention to your waist.

Once you've set aside your capsule wardrobe, go through all your other items with a fresh eye, seeing how they work with your basics. You'll be surprised at how many interesting and stylish combinations you'll come up with using your existing clothes.

Decluttering Your Closet

Now that you have your capsule wardrobe identified, it's time for the big clear-out! We've all told ourselves we really must sort out our old clothes and tidy our closets, but somehow it's one of those tasks we always put off for another day. So let's make today the day. And just in case you're still procrastinating, let me give you a list of reasons why you'll feel so much better once you've taken the plunge.

1. A slimmed-down closet streamlines your morning routine and takes the stress out of dressing.
2. The clothes you never wear won't be taking up precious space.
3. It'll be much easier to mix and match everything.
4. Everything you possess will be wearable—no more trying a pair of pants just in case you can miraculously now fit into them.
5. You'll be able to see at a glance what you have, so when you need a little retail therapy, it'll be easy to know what you purchase will enhance your wardrobe.
6. Chances are you'll have found one or two lovely items you completely forgot you owned, and now you can enjoy wearing them again.
7. The items you ultimately choose to donate go to a good cause and create a win-win situation.

8. If you have designer items in good condition, you can sell them through a consignment store.

What Stays and What Goes

Try asking yourself the following questions:

1. When did I last wear this? If it was more than a year ago, you should probably get rid of it.
2. How did I feel the last time I wore this? Did I feel fantastic (it's a keeper), or did I feel unattractive and awkward (get rid of it).
3. Would I buy it now if I saw it in the store? If you wouldn't, the chances are you won't wear it. Or if you do, you won't feel particularly good in it. If you try something on and hate it, you'll probably never fall in love with it again. And don't beat yourself up about it. We all make mistakes.
4. Is it in wearable condition? I know we all have those favorite items, but if it has a permanent stain or a tear that just can't be repaired, out with it!
5. Is this an expensive item to maintain? If it has to be dry-cleaned or ironed every time you wear it, is it worth the upkeep?
6. Will I *really* wear this again, or am I just hoping to wear it one day? Despite how much you love something in your wardrobe, if it doesn't fit, it's just time to let it go. Remember your height and body shape isn't going to miraculously change, nor are you going to grow younger, so if you're waiting for any of those to happen before you wear this again, get rid of it!

If you have seasonal clothes and closet space is limited, store them in suitcases or vacuum cubes (sold in Bed Bath & Beyond or online) and put them under the bed or in a less accessible clean, dry storage area. They'll keep until it's time to change out your wardrobe for the new season.

Organizing Hints

A closet is very valuable real estate. Don't waste it! A well-organized closet makes a great deal more space available to you and allows you to see what you have at a glance.

1. Keep your clothes in sections: dresses, tops, skirts, pants, etc. Store all your belts in the same spot, hang your sundresses alongside each other, and keep your workout clothes separate.

2. Color-code your sections. And not just your clothes. You can color-code your shoes and underwear and even your jewelry. It all saves time when you're getting dressed and will make selecting your outfit so much easier.

3. Storage baskets are your friend! Choose an attractive color. They'll look chic and keep all your loose "stuff" out of sight. They're great for rarely worn items like beach clothes, bathing suits, snow boots, etc. You can fit more in a tight place and still have everything organized. At the same time, you can put them on those higher, difficult-to-reach shelves. Label them, and you'll know exactly which basket to pull out when you're heading to the beach or snow.

4. Take advantage of your vertical storage space. Tops and pants only take half the height needed for dresses and coats, so you might be able to install a second closet rod.

5. An over-the-door shoe rack is a very useful item for turning a dead space into a valuable storage area.

6. Invest in space-saving hangers. Tiered hangers for skirts and pants are fantastic for maximizing hanging space. It's also worth getting rid of all your nasty, old, wire hangers and buying superthin hangers. They'll look much better and save even more space.

Think Outside the Box (or the Closet!)

There are some really great items you can repurpose to maximize your closet space. A trip to Ikea, the Container Store, Target, Walmart, etc. will provide you with some good storage items, but here are some ideas that you might not have thought of:

1. Shoe organizers are great for shoes of course, but you can also use them for sweaters, T-shirts, or jeans. Just roll them up and put them away in your organizer.

2. Utilize door and wall space. If you have unused wall space in your closet or bedroom, put up a pretty towel rail and use it to hang

scarves and belts. Just fold your scarves in half, feed them through the rod, and then pull the ends through their loops.

3. Magazine files (from Ikea, HomeGoods, etc.) are the ideal shape for storing clutch purses.
4. Hooks are a great asset when it comes to organizing your hats, scarves, and necklaces.
5. Small bookcases and cube shelving are great places for storing purses, shoes, accessories, and gym clothes.
6. Hardware storage (the kind with sixty drawers for nails and screws) are great for storing jewelry.

With a little creative thinking, the possibilities are infinite. Once you've sorted out your capsule wardrobe and decluttered your closet, make sure you don't slip back into bad habits. Practice closet maintenance. Keep a "discard bag" in your closet. Whenever you realize an item of clothing is past its prime, instead of hanging it up again, put it in your discard bag. Finally, try to stick with the one in/one out rule. If you buy something that isn't an essential item, get rid of one thing you really don't need. It might make you think twice before you make that impulse purchase. It also ensures decluttering is an ongoing process.

And just one final tip: use the power of perfume to make your closet even more attractive. Eliminate any musty odors by putting a few scented dryer sheets or sachets onto your shelves. Your closet and clothes will always smell fresh.

Chapter 7

JEWELRY

Never wear second-rate jewels, wait till the really good ones
come to you. Rather than a wretched little diamond full of
flaws, war a simple plainly inexpensive ring. In that case you
can say, "It's a memento. I never part with it, day or night."

—Colette

Accessories can make or break an outfit. One mistake I see a lot of women making is wearing too much jewelry or the wrong proportions—chunky jewelry with a soft, feminine outfit, for example. How do you know if you have on too much? Ask your mirror! Usually three pieces are sufficient: earrings, bracelet, and ring or earrings, necklace, bracelet. You get the idea. You may wear five or six pieces of jewelry to get a certain look. Remember there are no set rules. If done cleverly, you can mix gold and silver as well as chunky and delicate, but you have to know what you're doing. Too much is—well, too much!

The cost of your jewelry is not important. I enjoy wearing beautiful costume jewelry with an expensive dress or expensive real jewelry with a very inexpensive outfit. If you do wear costume jewelry, however, it should be of a good quality (secure clasps, finished well). Don't make the mistake of trying to pass off poorly made costume jewelry as real. Have fun with your fabulous fakes! As Coco Chanel said, "Costume jewelry is not made to give women an aura of wealth but to make them beautiful."

And *wear* your real jewelry. I have a friend who has a beautiful string of real pearls she keeps in her safe. What pleasure is there in that? To me, that's like locking a perfect rose in a room where no one will see or smell it. My two favorite pieces of real jewelry are necklaces: a cross I bought in Jerusalem and a Star of David that has a cross in the middle. Both items mean a lot to me because I've visited Jerusalem twice and they signify my love and respect for both Jews and Christians. Pearls are also a favorite of mine. I wear them often.

Capsule Jewelry

Just as it's good to build a capsule wardrobe of basic clothes, the same idea applies to jewelry. Do you have the elements that will enhance all your outfits, no matter how casual or dressy? Here's a useful guide for a good jewelry collection, and just remember fakes are fabulous!

- Pearl stud earrings. You can have both small, elegant pearls and large, chunky ones for fun.
- Diamond or cubic zirconia stud earrings. Always safe for a classy look.
- Hoop earrings, gold and silver. Again, you can go both large and small.
- Fun, versatile casual earrings.
- Dressy pendants.
- A pearl necklace. Try to wear a necklace that reflects the size of your pearl earrings. Chunky earrings should match a chunky necklace; fine pearls should be worn with a more delicate necklace.
- Diamond pendant necklace. Again, fake is fine!
- A bangle or chain bracelet.

When I talk about diamonds and pearls, I don't mean they have to be real. A fake diamond or pearl stud looks just as good. But remember it should be small enough that it *could* be real. These items are all about subtlety, not bling. You won't be alone if you're wearing fakes. Famous women who could easily afford the real deal have also had fun wearing flamboyant fakes. Style icons like Jackie Kennedy, Rihanna, Gwyneth Paltrow, and Beyonce have all been known to wear imitation jewels. Even our late First Lady Barbara Bush confessed to wearing fake pearls.

Now that we have the fundamentals covered, let's see how we can have fun with our jewelry—both real and fake. In the same way you worked on your capsule wardrobe, put on some of your favorite outfits and try various combinations of jewelry. You'll be surprised how many different looks you can achieve with the same basic outfit.

Necklaces

As we get older, there's no doubt that some necklaces just don't look as good. For instance, I think chokers are best avoided. They draw attention to the jawline, which might not be as firm and tight as it once was. Instead, I think pendants and long rope necklaces are far more flattering and elegant.

Coco Chanel believed in layering necklaces. Well, if it's good enough for the most influential woman in fashion, it's good enough for me! Experiment with contrasting lengths, shapes, textures, and colors to make an interesting statement. To begin, get out all necklaces and lay them side by side. Try putting together different combinations. It used to be a hard and fast rule that you never mixed metals like silver and gold, but that's no longer applicable.

Match your necklace to your neckline. If you're showing a little cleavage, for example, a necklace that sits in the V above your cleavage will look stunning. Don't wear a necklace that just hovers on the neckline of your garment. It looks messy. And if you're wearing something with a fussy collar or a busy pattern, it's probably best not wearing a necklace at all. This is a situation where less can be more.

And remember that real or fake, a string or two of pearls adds class to almost any outfit.

Bracelets

This is another area where you can mix and match. Again, get out all your bracelets and bangles and see what works together. I'm sure you'll find some surprising and stunning combinations.

Earrings

Remember when you're talking to someone, your earrings are in the field of vision, so they're a really important accessory. Your earrings should frame your face, complement your skin tone, look good with your hair style, and work with your top. Pendant earrings with a little sparkle are a quick and simple way to dress up an outfit. However, if your ear lobes are getting saggy, avoid earrings that are too heavy. They'll pull your lobes down and draw attention to the problem.

When in doubt, a simple pair of pearl earrings will always look good. Pearls are very flattering for every complexion and, whether clearly on display if you have short hair or just peeking through your hair if it's long, they add a little illumination to your face.

Rings

Diamonds may be a girl's best friend, but as I've indicated previously, they don't have to be real. Stacking rings are a great way to ring (!) the changes and add some color by mixing and matching different stones. But remember if you're going to be wearing rings that draw attention to your hands, make sure your hands are looking good. No ring, however gorgeous, will detract from chipped or bitten nails and unattractive, rough skin on your hands.

Bling

When I'm dressing for the stage, my jewelry has to be visible from a distance. I'll usually wear large earrings that catch the light, especially if my hair is down. But I still like my jewelry to be tasteful and not overdone. For example, if my top is beaded with long sleeves, I won't wear a bracelet. Really, I apply the same rules on stage as I follow for normal dressing, except a little bigger and brighter. Of course stage is different from TV, which is much more like normal wear.

Here are some thoughts on bling:

1. A necklace or earrings made of giant, fake pearls can look sensational.
2. If you're wearing a statement necklace and/or earrings, don't wear an armful of bangles. They'll compete for attention and distract from the impact you're trying to make.

3. If you're going for bling, make sure your outfit is simple. If you're wearing bold patterns, you might want to try more subtle jewelry.
4. Don't be too influenced by a friend or style icon who may look great with lots of bling. If you're uncomfortable with flash, ditch it!

Heirlooms

Inherited jewelry usually has great sentimental value. However, it doesn't always fit in with our clothes and lifestyle. But that doesn't mean you can't wear it. For example, a treasured pin doesn't have to be worn on a lapel. It can be used to fasten the top of a shirt or to hold a scarf in place.

Pearls are always classy, but some strings can look dated. However, if you add another necklace of a similar length, it can update a classic. Alternatively, you could take them to be restrung and add a more modern clasp, which will really switch them up.

Last thoughts: Just as you care for your clothes and shoes, do the same with your jewelry. Replace missing stones, and keep everything clean and polished.

And finally, have fun with your jewelry. All my suggestions are merely guidelines to help you maximize your accessories. But if you break the rules and the result is stylish or quirky and it makes you feel great, then go ahead. Enjoy!

Chapter 8

HATS

She had a passion for hats, none of which returned her affection.

—Storm Jameson, *The Intruder*

Hats are my absolute favorite accessory! Perhaps it's because I was raised in the east where a hat and gloves were required for church when I was a child. I do know that a hat can dramatically change the look of an outfit. Need to run to the store and your hair is a mess? Throw on a baseball cap and a pair of sunglasses. Put on some lip gloss, and you'll look like a movie star! I do that all the time. Wearing a plain old ho-hum dress to the luncheon? Put on a cute hat and voilà! A sophisticated outfit. I own many hats of different styles and materials. I even had a beautiful hat made to go with the gown I wore when I was a judge in the Miss Universe contest.

After I had been in The 5th Dimension for some years, I met a judge who remembered me from the days when I used to compete in beauty pageants. He told me one of the reasons I won the contest was because I was different. When the other contestants came out with lovely, elaborate gowns to show their talents, I came out in a white suit and a white hat, and I carried a large hat box. I sang "April in Paris" in French. Eartha Kitt turned to the other judges and said, "Now there's your winner." Could it have been the hat?

I wear big hats, small hats, bright colors—pretty much anything that catches my eye, looks good, and works with my existing outfits. It has been said that shorter women shouldn't wear large hats, but I do! Of course the whole outfit has to be balanced. If I wear a large hat, I will usually wear high heels. Again, it comes down to being comfortable with what you are wearing.

I enjoy my old habit of wearing a hat to church. As a matter of fact, when I occasionally go to church without one, everyone says, "Florence, where is your hat?" But remember to be considerate of others and don't wear a large hat to the theater or church where people will be sitting behind you and your hat will block their view. My favorite style of hat is a beret. I have tons of them in all different colors. They're not only versatile but so easy to pack.

I'm always surprised at the number of women who tell me they like my hats and would love to wear one but hats don't look good on them. I say that's nonsense. I believe it's just a matter of finding the right hat—one that looks good on you and that you feel comfortable in. Choose a style that complements your size and the shape of your face. Also consider the outfit you will be wearing and the occasion to which you will be wearing the hat. Have fun trying on hats and see what works best for you. As the famous hat designer Phillip Treacy said, "Try on one hundred different hats if you can, until you find the one that suits you best. It's a trial-and-error thing." The great news is they're the easiest item to try on in a store, so you can spend hours experimenting with different shapes, colors, and styles, and no one will disturb you.

Choosing the most flattering hat is like everything else with regards to style; take the time to find out what looks best for you. Before you head to the store or mall, study your face shape. It will help you choose which style of hat will flatter you the most.

Here's a guide:

- Long face: Make sure you choose a hat with a deep crown that you can wear quite low over your forehead. Wide brims and berets are especially flattering. Sarah Jessica Parker is a good example of a style icon with a long face. Although she often wears some pretty outrageous hats, you can find photos of her wearing less flamboyant creations that will show what clever hat choices she makes.

- Round face: Hats with asymmetrical brims will look great on you. Try wearing them slanted at interesting angles. Fedoras and flat caps are perfect for you. Actress Drew Barrymore has a round face and is a real hat girl! She particularly favors fedoras.
- Square face: Opt for a round hat that will contrast with your square jaw. Bowlers, fedoras, and beanies are particularly flattering. Demi Moore is a good example of this shape, as is Yoko Ono, who is rarely seen without a fedora and always looks stunning.
- Heart-shaped face: This is a good hat-wearing shape. Most hats will look good on you. Fedoras will always work, but you can be more adventurous and wear a cloche or pillbox. If you're not sure what a heart-shaped face looks like, Scarlett Johansson and Reese Witherspoon are perfect examples.
- Oval face: This is the easiest to suit. Pretty much anything will work. Oprah Winfrey and Angelina Jolie are both oval-faced celebrities. If you check out what they're wearing, it will work for you.

So now, taking into consideration the shape of your face, here are some tips I'd like to pass on to you. As a dedicated hat wearer, I know they'll make buying and wearing hats so much easier. Let's start off with a few dos and don'ts.

- Don't be intimidated by the thought of wearing a hat. It's just another accessory (and it can transform a bad hair day into a sensationally stylish look). There is a world full of hats out there to suit your style and personality.
- Wear your hat creatively. I've worn hats backward!
- Do wear a hat that's appropriate to the weather. I never understand how anyone can wear a knitted beanie on a blazing hot day; it looks so hot and uncomfortable. If beanies are your thing, wear a pretty crocheted or lace version during the summer months. And speaking of winter beanies, check out some alternatives to those woolen versions. They can be made out of luxurious cashmere as well as in bright colors and embellished with embroidered details like beading and sparkle.

- Do wear a hat that complements the mood of your outfit. If you're dressing for a casual event (or a trip to the market), don't wear a dressy hat with jeans. Conversely, beanies are casual and, as a general rule, shouldn't be worn with a business suit.
- Don't wear anything too busy with a hat, and don't wear too much heavy jewelry. Let your hat speak! The more flamboyant your hat is, the simpler your jewelry should be.
- Do make sure your hat fits properly. It should fit snugly and feel secure. If it's too loose, it will be floppy and uncomfortable. If it's too tight, it could give you a nasty headache.
- Do think outside the (hat) box! Hats can be whimsical and fun as well as elegant. They can turn the simplest outfit into a knockout. Make hats your own unique style statement.
- Do check out a leather baseball cap. It will elevate a pair of jeans and boots into something stunning.
- Do wear a straw hat with a pretty summer dress or flowing skirt. It always looks superfeminine. And if you want an extra flourish, you can put a ribbon that matches your dress around the crown.
- Do add some color interest with your hat if you're wearing an all-black outfit. A red hat and red shoes can transform a simple black pantsuit into a showstopper.
- Do try a newsboy cap or beret with a chunky sweater.
- Don't wear a sequined hat with a sequined dress, unless you're really going all out for a red-carpet look. One or the other is usually enough!
- Don't go over the top with your hats. You still want people to see your beautiful face not spend all their time looking at the top of your head!
- Do try a fedora in something other than black. Depending on your coloring, olive green, burgundy, gray, or camel can look great and still work with a black jacket or coat.
- Don't wear a big hat with a billowing, flowing dress. You'll disappear!
- Don't be afraid to wear a man's hat. Some of the best hats can be found in the menswear department. Adding a masculine touch to a feminine outfit is a classic, sexy look.

- Do keep your color palette simple and ensure your hat matches or complements at least one other item you are wearing.
- Check resale stores for interesting hats.

Hats and Hair

As I said earlier, hats are a great camouflage for a bad hair day or just a time when you don't feel like fussing with your hairdo. But you also have to consider the length of your hair and how to wear it under your hat.

If your hair is very short, try to have some of your hair peeking out from under your hat. On the other hand, if you have long, thick hair, don't always leave your hair hanging out from all sides. Also try tying it back in a neat bun or sleek ponytail at the nape of your neck. It will look quite elegant. When you wear a baseball cap, you can either tuck all your hair into it or gather your hair into a ponytail. Kate Middleton (the English duchess of Cambridge) is a perfect example of a woman who knows how to make sure her hat and hair work well together. The actress Catherine Zeta Jones is another Englishwoman who wears hats with great style and always gets her hair just right.

To summarize my feelings, hats are a perfect accessory for any outfit, anytime. In a flash, you can look stylish and put together, while guaranteeing that you'll never again have to worry about having a bad hair day. But most importantly, as celebrity hat maker Phillip Treacy says, *"How a hat makes you feel is what a hat is all about."*

Chapter 9

SHOES AND FEET

If high heels were so wonderful, men would be wearing them!

—Sue Grafton

As Cinderella discovered, one shoe can change your life! So is it any wonder why so many women are shoe nuts? I think it's also because shoes can make a personal statement about an outfit without shouting too loudly.

I used to own over one hundred pairs of shoes and boots, but most of them were ten years old (some even older). I've finally conquered my shoe fetish and haven't purchased a pair in almost a year. I've also given away all the shoes that didn't fit properly. Some of them were so beautiful and/ or expensive and hadn't been worn much, so it wasn't an easy thing to do. I was shocked and upset to discover that women wanted to pay only $2 to $3 at my garage sale for an expensive pair of shoes only worn once or twice. Needless to say, some of them ended up back in my closet.

Years ago, when The 5th Dimension first began, we used to have our shoes made. That was such a luxury. Believe me: no shoe is as comfortable as one that is custom made for you. Unfortunately, the shoemaker has since retired, and I haven't been able to find another anywhere in the United States. How I wish I had gotten my shoe last (a wooden form that cobblers use to make shoes).

I sometimes think that a crafty doctor must have designed the extremely high heels many women are wearing so he or she would have more patients. There have been more twisted ankles and backs thrown out of place than you can count, not to mention crushed toes and damaged toenails. Now I'm not saying there is anything wrong with being stylish and keeping up with the latest trends, but here again, one has to be sensible. If you don't have good balance or strong ankles, avoid extremely high heels. The pained look on your face as you try to walk in them is *not* attractive. And many of you remove your shoes after wearing them for an hour or so. What's the point in that? Why not wear a beautiful *comfortable* shoe? They really do exist. There are plenty of chic fashionable styles that have comfort soles and arch supports. I've finally come to my senses and cleared my closet of all shoes that don't fit properly so I won't be tempted to squeeze my poor feet into an instrument of torture! When I'm just relaxing around my house, I don't usually wear shoes. Rather, I wear a pair of thick socks in the winter or soft house slippers or thongs in the summer so my feet get a rest.

I used to wear heels every day, but now I wear cute flats. That way, I can enjoy wearing a higher heel for evening events as my feet are rested.

When I'm dressing for the stage, I buy shoes that fit properly so my feet never hurt after a performance. If my feet ever hurt, the shoes go, no matter how gorgeous they look. I once bought some shoes in a hurry without making really certain they were a good fit. I began performing in them but decided there was no point in pretending so I took them off while I was on stage. I'm quite certain there were many ladies in the audience who felt my pain! The only time I've worn flats on stage is after I had my hip surgery. It was more important for me to take care of my health while I performed than to wear high heels. But I did make sure my cane was covered in bling so I still had my glamorous accessory.

Capsule Wardrobe for Shoes

While I own a lot of shoes and boots, I've compiled a core wardrobe you could aim for. Of course, you might prefer more boots or more sandals, depending on the climate where you live or your particular lifestyle, but I've tried to come up with a fairly broad-based list that should work for most people. It will also help you to declutter your closet so you can get rid of those shoes you know you'll never wear again!

Here's my suggested list:

- Neutral pumps. They go with almost everything.

- Ballerina flats. They're comfortable and feminine. You can choose a neutral shade like black or go for a pop of color like red or pink.
- Classic loafers. Choose a neutral shade.
- Evening heels or sandals. Pick a pair in a shade that will match with as many of your evening dresses as possible, but I suggest you go with classic gold or silver hues that are more versatile.
- Knee-length boots.
- Ankle boots—preferably black, dark gray, or brown.
- Animal print heels. Well, a girl's entitled to some fun!
- Flat *strappy sandals*. They show off your pretty feet and can be worn with any summer garment from shorts to a floaty dress.
- Wedge sandals. They are always useful and never dated.
- Sneakers. Oh so comfortable, and they look great with jeans and pants. Now "fashionistas" are even wearing stylish sneakers with dresses. (Yay for comfort!)
- Last of all, something colorful in any style for those days when you just need to make a statement!

If these items are in your shoe closet, you'll never find yourself limping down the street in a pair of stilettos when you should be wearing flats just because they're the only ones that go with your chosen outfit. You'll have exactly the right shoes for any occasion.

I also like to make sure my shoe closet is carefully organized by color and style: dressy, casual, boots. That way, I can find exactly what I want immediately and not waste time rummaging through shelves and boxes.

Shoe Style

When it comes to style, I don't like shoes that have straps across the ankles because they break up the lines of the legs. I much prefer shoes that make the legs look longer. But that's my personal opinion, and as I'm petite, I think that works best for my height. Here are some more guidelines to wearing the best shoes for your body and for your outfit:

- Choose shoe colors that complement your clothes. They shouldn't be fighting for attention.

- If you're wearing a bold, bright pattern, wear simple black or neutral heels or flats. Or if you want to go with color, choose one from the pattern.
- If you want to add a pop of color, wear a brightly colored shoe with a simple black dress.
- It's not necessary to be too *matchy matchy,* but it can work.
- Animal print shoes are always a great way to add pizzazz to a neutral outfit.
- Make sure your shoes fit the season. Sandals are great for summer; heavy boots are not!

Shoe Size and Fit

Don't try to squeeze your feet into a size seven when you know you need an eight! Most of us have one foot that is larger than the other, so buy the larger size and have your shoe repairer adjust the smaller shoe. Fortunately, I have a very good shoe repairer who will change heels on shoes or adjust a strap to make my shoes fit better. He's really my shoe tailor.

Many women wear the wrong size shoes. Our foot sizes change as we go through life. For example, many women's feet become a half or a full size larger after having a baby. My feet are a full size larger than before I was pregnant. Oh, the many beautiful pairs of shoes and boots I had to get rid of! You should also check the size of your shoes when you lose or gain weight, as it most likely will change.

While I like to bargain hunt for clothes and accessories, I won't skimp on shoes. Rarely have I found inexpensive shoes that fit me properly because, like most women, I have two different-size feet, which are also shaped differently. It doesn't matter how beautiful your outfit is; if your feet hurt, the whole look is ruined. Although I prefer high heels (three inches), I've been advised by my podiatrist to vary the height of my heels during the day. If I wear flat shoes, I make sure they have good arch supports, or my feet will hurt.

Bearing all this in mind, here are a few tips to ensure that the shoes you love love your feet:

1. Believe it or not, it's best to shop for shoes during the afternoon. Your foot naturally expands during the day, so it will prevent you squeezing into the wrong size.
2. Make sure your socks or pantyhose are the same as you'll wear with you shoes after you've bought them. If you wear thin pantyhose and try on shoes that you'll normally wear with socks, you'll end up with very cramped toes.
3. Make sure the shoes fit well on both feet. As I explained before, your foot size will change with age and feet are rarely the same size.
4. And remember shoe sizes vary from manufacturer to manufacturer. Don't be fooled by numbers. Go for fit.
5. Take your time when you're buying shoes. Walk around in them. You should have about a half inch of space between your longest toe and the end of the shoe so there's enough room for your foot to press forward as you walk. Wiggle your toes to make sure there's plenty of space to move.
6. Good fit isn't just about length; it's about width too. Your toes shouldn't feel as though they're being squashed.

Foot Care

A lot of people neglect their feet, which is a big mistake. There are over seven thousand nerve endings in each foot, and they have the important task of bearing the weight of your entire body. That's a lot of potential pain! Corns, calluses, and blisters can very quickly develop, not to mention more long-term problems like hammertoes and bunions. Think of it this way: our feet are the workhorses of our bodies. But we cram them into high heels, squash them into tight pantyhose, and suffocate them in sweaty socks. And then we walk, jump, dance, and stand on them for hours on end. No wonder they rebel! It's also worth noting the knock-on effect of foot problems. If, for instance, you have a painful bunion, you'll try to take the weight of it by altering your walk. Ultimately, that will affect your back and leg joints, causing you even more pain.

The good news is there are lots of simple ways to take care of your feet without even setting foot (!) in a salon or podiatrist's office. Let's start with some simple foot care. After all, smelly feet and dirty, cracked heels are never acceptable.

- Wash your feet daily, using a pumice stone to exfoliate if necessary. Then make sure you dry them thoroughly, especially between the toes. This will reduce the likelihood of problems, such as athlete's foot and fungus. But beware. Never use a pumice stone on injured or sore areas.
- Keep your toenails trimmed straight across.
- Wear clean socks or pantyhose every day.
- Moisturize your feet. Use a foot cream, body lotion, or oil.
- When you have time, give your feet a spa treatment. Soak them in hot water for ten minutes. (You can add some perfumed oil or bubble bath for extra luxury.) Then scrub your heels with a pumice stone or foot brush. That will get rid of any ingrained dirt and leave your feet soft and fragrant. If you do this at night, rub some Vaseline into your feet and put on some light cotton socks so your skin will absorb the moisture overnight.
- If your feet are tired and aching, pour half a cup of Epsom salt into a footbath of warm water. Soak them for about ten minutes, dry them carefully, and then massage them with lavender or rosemary essential oils.
- Before putting on your athletic socks and going to the gym or for a long walk, rub plenty of moisturizer into your feet. Your feet will have a nice, little moisturizing steam bath while you're getting fit.
- To make your own foot scrub, dilute two tablespoons of sea salt into equal amounts of baby oil and lemon juice, then rub gently into your feet and rinse off.

Foot Exercises

I also do exercises to strengthen my feet and ankles, which ensure the muscles are providing the best support. Here are a few you can try. They can all be done sitting on a chair.

1. Try to pick up small marbles with your toes.
2. Put a towel on the floor, and try pulling it toward you with your toes.
3. Roll your ankles clockwise then counterclockwise ten times each.

4. Put your feet flat on the floor, then, keeping your toes on the floor, raise your heels. Stop when only the balls of your feet remain on the ground. Hold this position for five seconds before lowering the heels. Repeat ten times.

5. Spread your toes apart as far as possible without straining. Hold the position for five seconds. Repeat ten times.

There are many other exercises you can find online (or a professional can show you) for strengthening your feet and ankles.

Footnote

One of the best things you can do for your feet is reflexology. This is a type of massage used to relieve tension and treats illnesses, based on the theory that there are reflex points on the feet, hands, and head that are linked to specific organs, glands, and other parts of the body. Practitioners of reflexology believe that pressure can promote health in corresponding organs through energetic pathways. I've found this type of "massage" very helpful, and it feels good too!

No matter how gorgeous your shoes and feet may be, remember your legs are on show so you need to ensure they look their best too. To prevent or reduce veins in your legs, elevate! Lie with your butt against a wall and put your legs straight up the wall. Lie there for ten minutes and relax. If that's too hard at first, just lie on the floor and elevate your legs on a chair. And if you're watching TV, sit with your legs up on a chair or table, with a cushion underneath them.

If you have veins on your legs and you're self-conscious, try using self-tanning creams. A little bronze can conceal a lot. The best kind is a moisturizer with a self-tanning element.

Chapter 10

DRESSING FOR THE BIG OCCASION

etting ready for a big event is all about preparation. First I assemble everything I'm going to wear—dress, shoes, undergarments, jewelry, etc.—at least a week in advance to make sure everything fits comfortably and is clean, pressed, and ready to be worn. On the day of the event, I allow myself at least two hours to get ready. I start by taking a long, luxurious hot bath. Then I put on my makeup. The most important thing for me is eye makeup, and that takes the longest because of the fake lashes. About thirty minutes. I listen to music and do everything in a very leisurely manner, so I'm not stressed when I have to leave. I like to be well rested so I can enjoy the event.

When I'm dressing up, I want something glamorous, elegant, and feminine, an outfit that makes me feel good. My favorite special occasion dress is a beautiful strapless gown in emerald green. It has a heavily sequined bodice and simple skirt. I'm actually thinking that I will probably have my seamstress add sleeves to it, as I don't think I want to go strapless at the moment. I also have a matching sequined hat. Another favorite is a simple, purple gown with a sequined bodice and see-through sleeves. I love wearing these gowns because I know they complement me and they're comfortable. When it comes to choosing colors for special occasion dressing, I have no particular favorites. I love colors, but I wear lots of black too. I like to dress appropriately for any event. For example, if I'm receiving an award, I want to achieve that "star" look.

When it comes to accessories, I don't think everything has to match, as long as the items complement each other in color and style. I also try to wear some more adventurous color combinations; red and green are colors

I like together. I usually wear gold accessories because they look better with my skin tone, but I do wear silver when I feel it's more suitable for the outfit I'm wearing.

Guidelines for Special Occasion Dressing

When we receive invitations for special events, there's often an indication of appropriate dress code. But sometimes, even that can be confusing. So here are some suggestions for what kind of clothes to wear when:

- Cocktail attire. Wear a knee or midcalf dress in almost any fabric. The classic little black dress is perfect here if you want to be supersafe. You can also opt for a dressy jumpsuit or tuxedo-type pantsuit. Cocktail attire is usually required for evening social events.

- Lounge. A pretty day dress is appropriate—nothing glitzy or low-cut. Loungewear is usually the dress code for daytime engagement parties, business breakfasts or lunches, and afternoon tea.

- Black tie: A floor-length evening gown. You can pull out all the stops for this kind of event, which would include charity fundraisers, award ceremonies, and evening weddings.

- Warm-weather black tie. A long dress, but you can wear something really feminine and floaty in a fabric like chiffon or lace. If it's a summer black-tie event, you might be in a garden or tent, so bring a warm, pretty wrap with you just in case. Goosebumps are not an attractive accessory! And remember, if you might be walking on grass, a pair of dressy flats is probably better to wear than spiky high heels.

- Black tie optional. This can be tricky. You can wear a long gown, cocktail dress, or very dressy separates like a tuxedo suit. If you're nervous about being over- or underdressed, wear a simple outfit and accessorize with some bling. Black tie optional is often the dress code for weddings and formal dinners.

When in doubt, keep it simple.

Shopping for a Special Event

If you're going to be shopping for something new for a special event, there's more to consider than just the dress code. Take a good look at yourself and decide which part of your body is your best asset so you can show it off. If you have great shoulders, go strapless. Maybe your legs are your pride and joy. In which case, look for a skirt that will reveal them when you move. But be careful of that thigh-high split. Perhaps you like to show a little (and I mean a little) cleavage. Once you've decided that, it will help you hone in on the perfect outfit. The most important thing you want to feel is *great*.

Here are some things to consider when you hit the stores:

1. It might be helpful to check out what your particular style icon has worn for a similar event. Of course, you don't want to copy an Oscar-worthy dress and wear it to your daughter's wedding, but check out the silhouette, color, accessories, etc. It might help you focus on what to look for if you're shopping for something new.

2. Don't spend a fortune on a dress you're going to wear once. Resale and discount shops are a great resource.

3. The alternative to buying something you'll only wear once is to find a great-fitting, elegant, simple outfit and accessorize, accessorize, accessorize! If, like most people, you don't go to black-tie events too often, choose a really simple little black dress to form the basis of your look. You can have such fun accessorizing with jewelry, shoes, a purse, and a wrap.

4. Don't buy anything too tight or too short. Make sure your outfit fits. A form-fitting dress looks lovely; a tight dress can be distinctly unlovely. Also, you want to be able to sit down without your dress splitting or revealing too much thigh.

5. We all know you can never go wrong with a black outfit, but don't be afraid of color. Just make sure you know what's best for your skin tones.

6. Look at your outfit from *all* angles. If you're circulating round a room, you need to look just as good from behind as in front.

7. Try to look for an outfit that has some interesting details and features. Something simple like a lace panel, a few sequins, or some beading around the neckline or sleeve can make all the difference.

8. Consider the weather. If you're wearing a stunning sleeveless outfit on a cold day, don't spoil the look by throwing an old coat over it or shivering your way through the evening because you didn't bring anything appropriate to wear over it. Find a pretty wrap that coordinates with your outfit. They're not too expensive and can be used again and again.

9. If the dress requirement is a once-in-a-lifetime full ball gown that you know you'll never wear again, try renting.

10. Look for versatility. Consider how your chosen purchase will look with different accessories. Can you dress it up or down? Can you change the color of your accessories to give the outfit a new look?

11. Try to shop well in advance of the event. If it's important enough to be buying something new, you want to have plenty of time to choose the perfect item and accessories. Shopping for something special at the last minute is far too stressful.

12. Special event dressing isn't like dressing for every day. Be open to new possibilities. Try on colors and styles that are a little bit outside of your comfort zone. You might surprise yourself.

13. Do the sit test. If you can't sit in the dress in the changing room, you won't be able to sit in it at the event!

14. If separates are appropriate for the event you'll be attending, don't overdo the bling. If you're choosing an elaborate top in a shiny metallic fabric or covered in beads or sequins, opt for simple dress pants or skirt in velvet or silk.

15. When in doubt, get a second opinion. If you don't have a trusted friend with you, either take a photo of yourself in the outfit and send it to her, see what the store's return policy is, or as a last resort, check out someone in the fitting room you consider has good taste and ask her opinion.

How to Look "Star"

That extra special event deserves some extra attention to detail.

- Accessories are key to special event dressing. They can take an outfit from good to spectacular in an instant. When you're shopping for accessories, take your outfit with you. It will help with color choices, whether you're trying to match a shade, contrast, or even pick out one color from a patterned fabric. Sometimes, we think one color is dominant and decide to use that as the base for our accessories but suddenly discover there's another shade that will work much better.

- I've discussed shoes at length in another chapter, so I won't repeat myself here. Just remember if you're going to be wearing shoes you already own, you want them in tip-top condition. Make sure they aren't scuffed or worn looking. No matter how gorgeous your dress is, sad shoes will detract! And if you're wearing new shoes, make sure you've broken them in. Pain is not compatible with that star glow!

- If your outfit doesn't fit perfectly, go to a tailor to make the necessary alterations. For example, if your dress has spaghetti straps, you want them to fit comfortably, not slip off your shoulders every time you move. Make sure you allow plenty of time for alterations. Dropping a dress off the night before just won't do. Allow two or three weeks to make sure everything gets done properly and in time.

- Shapewear is a girl's best friend for occasion dressing.

- Creases are not "star"! Carefully iron or steam your outfit and hang it carefully so it will be red carpet ready for you to slip into.

- Don't try something new on the night of your event! If you're going to wear bolder makeup or fake lashes, practice first. You might find it really doesn't work as well as you thought. Special occasion makeup can be more daring than you would wear every day, but it shouldn't be over-the-top.

- Photograph yourself in the outfit ahead of time. That way, you can see immediately if anything doesn't look or fit right.

- If your dress or top has to go over your head, keep a scarf handy. Once you have your makeup done and you're ready to get dressed, put the scarf over your head, covering your face. Then pull on your dress or top over the scarf. You'll prevent any makeup from getting on your clothes.

And one final "star" tip: No matter how much you love your huge daytime purse that contains everything you need in life, it just isn't appropriate for a dressy event. A small clutch is definitely called for. But don't panic. Here's a list of essential items I suggest you take with you. Eliminate everything else!

- Mints. You can never be confident without fresh breath.
- The smallest hairbrush or comb that will work for your hair.
- A couple of safety pins. They can save the day in the event of a broken strap or torn hem.
- A little cash to hand out for tips in the ladies' room.
- A credit card in case of emergency.
- Lipstick and gloss.
- A Band-Aid or two in case those new shoes aren't quite the perfect fit. You still want to be able to dance the night away.
- Eye drops. So useful if it's getting late, you're tired, but you still want your eyes to sparkle.
- A pack of tissues.
- Stain-removing pen—just in case. Crowded events, especially the crowded cocktail hour when everyone is circulating, can be disaster areas when you're trying to juggle a glass of wine and a stuffed mushroom!

Week before Prep

Star quality isn't just about the clothes and makeup. In order to look your best on the night, prepare your body for a few days beforehand. I don't mean you should go on a starvation diet. Just try to cut down on any foods that make you bloat. No salt or alcohol is allowed if you want to look truly "star." Drink lots of water every day to cleanse your body.

Lots of celebrities get expensive teeth-whitening treatments before red-carpet events. But you don't need to do that. Just invest in a packet of Crest White Strips. Once you've given yourself a whitening treatment, avoid coffee, tea, or anything else that might stain your teeth (like berries).

And now the easiest advice of all for you to follow at the big event: go and have fun!

Chapter 11

MAKEUP AND SKIN CARE

Almost always it is the fear of being ourselves
that brings us to the mirror.

—Antonio Porchia

The three most common makeup mistakes I see are wearing too much, women copying a look they see a model in a magazine wearing (many don't realize that the heavily made-up models in magazines are often presented that way to sell a product), and sporting the latest makeup craze and hues with no regard to their own coloring and facial structure.

For older women, wearing too much makeup just adds years to our looks. Often the makeup just settles in the facial lines and accentuates them. I know that after I put my makeup on, I often wipe some of it off (unless I'm applying it for stage). When I'm not performing, I just wear moisturizer, eyebrow pencil (because my brows are thin from overplucking them), and mascara. I may use a tinted moisturizer, lip gloss, eyeliner on my upper eyelid and add a little blush if I'm going to a meeting. If I date someone I expect will be "a keeper," I like to wear as little makeup as possible, so when he sees my naked face at the beach, he won't be shocked! All this I can do in about fifteen minutes. When I attend a special event, or if I just want to look "star," I wear false lashes. It takes me about an hour to put on my stage makeup, because I like a very dramatic look, and my eye makeup takes longer to apply.

When young girls wear too much makeup, it makes them look loose and erases the fresh, dewy look of youth. Personally, I don't think a girl should wear makeup until she is sixteen. (Hey! I'm old-fashioned!) Then all she needs is moisturizer and lip gloss. At eighteen, she can begin to add eye makeup. These days, young girls begin wearing makeup at ten and eleven years old, and by the time they reach sixteen, they look like women. Then we wonder why there is so much sexual aggression in our young people and why so many girls are approached by older boys and men. Girls are not allowed to enjoy their youth. (Then, when they become women, they try to recapture it. Isn't that ironic?) I realize the pressure put on young girls by magazines, cosmetic companies, and their peers. I remember being very embarrassed when my mother caught me, at fifteen, wearing lipstick to church and told me (in front of my friends), "Wipe that lipstick off your lips, young lady." My mother never had to do it again. I was blessed to be occupied with so many other things (caring for my sisters, sports, and reading) that the incident soon passed. Besides, I knew someone would tell her if I did it again, and very few of my friends were allowed to wear makeup, so I wasn't the odd one out. I did look forward to the day when I would be allowed to wear that coveted lipstick!

It's fun to experiment with new makeup ideas and colors. This has led me to make some mistakes, like wearing far too much makeup on occasions. Now, however, I've discovered that the older I get, the less makeup I wear, the better (and younger!) I look. Go figure!

The general rule with makeup is to enhance your best feature and play down the rest of your face. For instance, I do heavy eye makeup, so I wear a lighter lipstick. For stage, or some evenings, I will break that rule. I just go all out with heavy eye makeup and red lips. You have to experiment to find what works for *you*. And again, what is appropriate for the occasion. I like the makeup and the clothes of the 1940s, so I'll often adopt that look when appropriate.

But before we get into the details of makeup, we should take a look at skin care. No matter how creative we are with foundation, eye shadow and brushes, we need to make sure the canvas beneath is in good condition, with a healthy glow and clear surface.

Skin Care

Our faces tell a story. After all, we've earned every single one of our lines. As fashion guru Diane von Furstenberg said, "My face carries all my memories. Why would I erase them?" And that's absolutely true. But I come from a generation of women who smoked, neglected their diet, and would spend hours sunbathing while slathered in baby or coconut oil, never thinking (or knowing) about sun protection factor. So while we don't want to obliterate our past, we do need to correct some of the negative influences. It's never too late to use sunblock, stop smoking, and improve your diet. We can also minimize the appearance of lines and try to prevent more from forming.

The skin is a huge organ, measuring an area of approximately twenty feet. Just like the heart, liver, kidneys, brain, etc., it needs to be maintained and kept healthy. Fortunately, the healthier you are, the better your skin will look. Without good nutrition, plenty of sleep, and regular exercise, even the most expensive moisturizer and makeup will fail to give you that youthful radiance. Here are some tips to improve your skin from the *inside:*

1.   Detox days are a good way to add some glow to your skin. Try having the occasional day during which you restrict your diet to raw fruit and vegetables only. And use those days to detox the outside of your skin too. Cleanse and moisturize your skin, then leave it makeup free for the day.
2.   Maintain good circulation through regular exercise.
3.   Keep your alcohol intake to a minimum.
4.   Take a daily dose of flaxseed oil or olive oil. They both have plenty of omega-3 fatty acids that lubricate the skin.
5.   Drink lots of water every day.

Now we can take a look at the *outside,* or skin surface. For good skin, cleanse, cleanse, cleanse, moisturize, moisturize, moisturize! I can't emphasize this enough.

Particularly for those of us living in polluted urban cities, cleansing is an essential part of any beauty routine. Never ever go to bed wearing your makeup. It's one of the most aging things you can do. You also need to know your skin type so you can choose the correct cleanser for your face.

You don't want to use anything too harsh, just a mild cleanser that will dissolve dirt and makeup. And exfoliate your face once or twice a week. Be sure not to use too hot water. I use lukewarm to cool water, ending with cold water to close my pores. And don't scrub your face! Wash by using gentle, upward, and circular motions. Scrubbing pulls on the skin, creating sagging and accelerating aging.

As for *washing* your face, too much washing strips the skin's natural oils while washing too infrequently can cause acne. Although I have oily skin, I only wash my face in the evening. In the morning, I just splash gently with cold water. At night, I first use a mild eye makeup remover and then a premoistened towelette to remove my makeup, if I am wearing any. If I am wearing stage makeup, I may use two towelettes to ensure thorough removal. I then gently wash my face with barely warm water, finishing with cold water. I just discovered a cleansing mousse by Caudalie that I like very much. It's a bit pricy, but it lasts a long time and is, I think, worth the cost. There are lots of other inexpensive cleansers that are probably just as good. My grandmother used nothing but Ivory soap, and her skin was beautiful, but I'm not sure that's the best beauty advice!

Those of you who, like I, are blessed with oily skin must be careful not to use on your face heavy moisturizers that will clog your pores. I suggest you try several products and select the one that works best for you. Face oils are very effective if you have dry skin. Remember to use your chosen oil sparingly, and warm it in the palm of your hand before you gently massage it into your skin. Sophia Loren has mentioned in several interviews that she uses olive oil. When I met her, she had her hair pulled back and wore very little visible makeup, and she was *stunning!* Clearly, the olive oil method works for her.

Whatever kind of cleanser, moisturizer, serum, or oil you're using, make sure you always apply it in an upward and outward movement. It really does help counteract gravity. Use gentle, sweeping movements, working from the center of your face outward. In the short term, it gets the circulation going, helps products melt into the skin, and feels soothing. In the long term, it minimizes the downward pull. If you follow this rule, you're subtly lifting the face every time you apply your skin care products.

Face masks are fantastic! There are so many available now. And try alternating different types—exfoliating, brightening, nourishing, deep cleansing, etc.—so all your skin care needs will be addressed.

When flying, don't wear makeup. Slather on lots of moisturizer (coconut oil is particularly good) throughout the journey. When you get to your destination, exfoliate, and use a moisturizing face mask. You'll look as though you've just had a day at the spa instead of a long-haul flight!

Makeup

When I perform on television or in a show or have a photo shoot where a makeup artist is hired, I allow him or her to make me up so I can learn new techniques and update my look. But I tactfully forewarn them that there are certain things about my makeup that I am particularly comfortable with and I may change what they have done. For instance, I like my eyebrows arched more than most makeup artists will consider correct. I assure them this does not mean that I don't think they are good at what they do, and I'm still open to new ideas. As a result of this honesty, I have been able to retain my signature "look" over the years and still appear current.

When it comes to makeup, try different products and looks to find out what feels right for you. Let your mirror be your guide, and be honest with yourself. If you need some advice, check out the department stores. They often have makeup experts from beauty houses who will do a makeup session for nothing. Of course, they want you to buy their products, but there is no rule that says you have to! Just getting a mini makeover will give you some idea of what you can change about your own routine. Also, there are lots of online tutorials you can check out.

As I've said, I belong to the "less is more" school when it comes to makeup for older women. I know that as I get older, the less makeup I wear, the better I look.

For a minimalist look, here is a quick and simple routine to have you looking good in a few minutes:

1. Foundation and blusher are the basic elements to have you looking your best instantly. They camouflage uneven skin tone and give you a healthy, youthful glow. If you want less coverage, try a tinted moisturizer.

2. Make sure your brows are well shaped and have some color. If, like mine, they're sparse, define them with an eyebrow pencil.

3. If you want to enhance your eyes a little, apply some smoky eye shadow to your lids. You might prefer to use a light powder instead of a pencil as a pencil might pull on your skin. If you do prefer pencil, use a very soft one. Chunky eye shadow pencils are good for this.

4. An eyelash curler is a great addition to your beauty collection. Apply mascara after curling, making sure there are no clumps.

5. Apply a light coat of lipstick or lip gloss. That little bit of color really brightens the face.

Now there's no excuse to leave the house without your "face" on!

Problems—and Solutions

As we age, there are some common problems that emerge.

1. Dark skin around the eyes is a common problem often caused by too little sleep. If this is a constant issue, make sure you stay hydrated and apply slices of chilled cucumber or cold tea bags to the area. Color-correcting primers also work well to conceal any discoloration.

2. Crepey eyelids occur as we get older and this delicate skin gets thinner and stretchy. Use a serum and a moisturizer on your lids, and be sure to be very delicate when you're removing your eye makeup. It's tempting to rub hard when that stubborn mascara won't disappear, but just take your time.

3. A good primer will work wonders if you have greasy eyelids. It will stop your eye shadow from smudging and looking messy. Panda eyes are only attractive on a panda!

4. If you have hooded eyes, apply eye shadow as follows: a lighter color on the brow bone, a darker shade in the socket line, and a light shade on the eyelid. Gently blend them to create a subtle effect, which will give depth to your eyes.

5. Use a soft eyebrow pencil or use a root touch-up product with a wand application to deal with loss of eyebrows.

6. Bristly, wayward eyebrow hairs should be plucked and trimmed. Sometimes you can contain them with a clear coat of false eyelash glue.

7. For thinning eyelashes, you can create the illusion of thicker lashes by applying the shadow into the roots of your lashes. This will create a soft, subtle line that will make your lashes seem thicker. For special occasions, I use strip false eyelashes. You can also have individual lashes added professionally.

Makeup Maintenance

How old is your makeup? If that sounds like a silly question, I can assure you it isn't. Believe it or not, some makeup shouldn't be kept more than three months, while others last a couple of years. Unfortunately, here in the US, there are no laws requiring manufacturing companies to include an expiration date on the packaging. But the fact is, makeup expires and can become a breeding ground for bacteria. All makeup should be kept in a cool, dry place with the lids tightly closed. Below is a guide showing how long different products last:

- mascara and liquid eyeliner: three to six months
- eye pencil: one year
- blush, eye shadow, and other powder cosmetics: one to two years
- liquid foundations and liquid or cream makeup: six months
- powder foundations and powder-formulated makeup: two years
- face lotions and eye creams: three months to one year
- lipstick: eighteen months to two years
- sunscreen: six months
- natural products: three to six months (If you use natural, preservative-free cosmetics, remember they have a shorter shelf life. If you store them in your refrigerator, they'll last a little longer.)
- makeup brushes: wash every two to three months
- makeup sponges: 1 month

Purchasing Makeup

It's not necessary to purchase expensive makeup. Health nut that I am, I usually buy natural, hypoallergenic makeup, which does tend to be a bit pricy. This is necessary for me, because my eyes tend to be allergic to certain ingredients in some makeup. However, most cosmetics that can be bought at the drugstores are fine for the majority of women. Choose the ones that work best for you and your budget. There are so many skin care products available in all different price ranges. Target, for example, has a great range of inexpensive beauty products. Also check online sales. You can often get great deals with bonus offers.

When you're buying makeup, make sure you test the colors the correct way. Swipe lipstick on your thumb and foundation, and test concealer and shadow in the web between thumb and forefinger. Always try the product out on skin similar to the area where it will be used. The web of skin near your thumb is thinner, looser, and crinkled; it will show how face makeup or eye shadow will look when applied. The same area is also more like actual lip skin and gives a truer idea of lipstick shade and texture. Testing lipstick on the back of your hand, as most of us do, actually gives a false color impression.

And the Rest ...

And ladies, as we're talking skin, don't forget to moisturize those areas of the body that aren't visible (thighs, feet, etc.). If you are single and God blesses you with a mate, you don't want to have to go on a mission to soften those heels so you won't snag your expensive sheets or—worse—scratch your spouse.

My body is like butter from head to toe. When I was recently in the hospital for some routine tests, the doctor commented on my soft skin. Who knows? That might be how I meet the man God has chosen for me for a husband. He may be a doctor! And single people, do it for yourselves.

I admit I'm guilty of taking too many long, hot, bubble baths. I know this can rob the body of its natural oils and can contribute to dry skin, but I always find this pleasant ritual so relaxing. If you feel the same way, don't indulge more than twice a week. It's better to incorporate daily showers and washing. Use a skin-moisturizing bath gel (I like Neutrogena's Rainbath) and afterward, apply body lotion while your skin is damp to get the most effect.

Chapter 12

HANDS

No matter how youthful our faces may be, no matter how much care we take to keep our bodies in shape, no matter how stylishly we dress, our hands are often the giveaway to aging. In fact, they can sometimes be the first part of our bodies to show signs of those advancing years.

Unfortunately, the skin on our hands can become wrinkled and crepe-like because of fat loss and collagen depletion. That's why the veins often seem more prominent on older hands; there's no plump cushion of fat and collagen to conceal them. While we can never truly reverse this, there are plenty of ways to slow down the process and improve the appearance of our hands. Additionally, we can employ a few good tricks that will, as the old song goes, "Accentuate the positive, eliminate the negative, latch on to the affirmative …"

Skin Care
- The first rule of hand care is *wear gloves!* Washing dishes and doing general housecleaning using hot water and abrasive detergents strips away all the natural oils from your skin.
- Now that that's out of the way, the next rule is to moisturize. Our hands are in and out of water more than any other part of our body, but while we slather creams on our face, arms, and legs, we often forget about those poor hands. They need plenty of TLC; they've earned it. Look for hand creams containing ingredients like shea butter, olive oil, vitamin E, and macadamia nut oil. The good news is they're present in very inexpensive brands like Eucerin Plus

Intensive Repair Hand Cream, Lubriderm Advanced Therapy Hand Cream, and Nivea Smooth Indulgence Hand Cream, all readily available at the drugstore. Apply the cream to slightly damp hands. It will seal in the moisture on the surface of your skin and absorb better. Keeping jars or tubes of hand cream close to all your sinks (kitchen and bathroom) will serve as a reminder for you to use them whenever your hands get wet.

- Sunspots develop over the years as a result of exposure to UV rays (or tanning beds if you used them). There are creams available to reduce their appearance, but you need to talk to your dermatologist for recommendations. Whether you have age spots or not, prevent more from appearing by using sunscreen. Yes, applying sunscreen to your hands is just as essential as putting it on your face, but so often we neglect this part of skin care. And don't forget to reapply after washing your hands. If you're self-conscious about your sunspots, you can apply a thin layer of opaque concealer or use a self-tanning lotion. It won't make them disappear but will reduce the appearance.

- Few of us think about exfoliating our hands, but if done regularly, it removes dirt, germs, and dead skin from the surface, allowing for better absorption of moisturizing creams. Just like your face, dead skin cells make your skin look flaky and dull. Use a gentle exfoliator—the same one you use on your face—then apply lots of moisturizer. Or for a simple and luxurious home treatment, warm coconut or olive oil and massage it into your hands for five to ten minutes. If you have a little more time to spare, put cotton-lined gloves over your hands after the massage and keep them on for thirty minutes or so. Then, rinse off the oil. Your hands will feel fantastic.

- If you feel like splashing out (or your birthday is coming up!), you could treat yourself to a paraffin wax hand bath. There are several small units for home use that won't break the bank. They're fantastic for really deep-moisturizing treatments that coat the skin.

- Exercise and massage your hands. It's easy to forget that our finger and wrist joints, just like all our other joints, stiffen as we get older. Regularly exercising your hands and massaging your joints is a great way to maintain flexible, pain-free joints. There are some very good online instruction videos available to show you the best techniques.

Nail Care

Keep your hands well-manicured. Chipped nail polish, ragged cuticles, and dry skin will detract from any efforts you may have made with your skin care and styling. That doesn't mean going to the salon every week. You can do it yourself at home.

Giving yourself a professional-looking manicure is simple.

- Remove existing nail polish.
- Trim and file your nails. Dragon lady nails don't look good on older hands, so don't leave your nails too long.
- Massage in some cuticle oil, leaving it to absorb for a few minutes.
- Gently push your cuticles back with a cuticle pusher. Never cut your cuticles, as this can cause bleeding and leave you vulnerable to infections.
- Clean your nail surface with a little rubbing alcohol before applying a base coat.
- Apply base coat.
- Apply nail varnish.
- Apply topcoat.
- If you want to give your nails a break from nail polish but still want them to look "polished," apply a nail strengthener like Sally Hansen Hard as Nails, which comes in clear or natural tint.

A final thought on nails: Dark or black nail polish or extravagant nail art might be tempting, but they don't necessarily look good on older hands. Choosing the right shade, whether you prefer a pop of color or pale neutrals, will give you a youthful, stylish look.

Rings

When you're choosing a ring, whether it's a potential heirloom or a fun piece of bling, it's a good idea to consider the length and width of your finger and the shape of your hand before you make your selection. It's also worth considering how you usually wear your nails. Are they trimmed short or long and manicured?

Long fingers: Try princess cut and round stones, wider bands. You can also be adventurous with your style, wearing chunkier or bolder designs than those of us with smaller hands.

Slender fingers: Even if they're long, they might be overwhelmed by something too large. Go for smaller stones, but you can still wear wider bands.

Short fingers: To give the illusion of length, opt for oval, pear, or marquise stones. Stay away from bands that are too wide. Choose narrow, delicate ones instead.

Wide fingers: Oval, marquise, rectangular, or emerald shapes will work best for you, keeping with narrow stones. Try clusters of stones too, and choose medium or thick bands. Angular and asymmetrical designs will make your fingers look slimmer.

Big knuckles: Thicker, heavier bands will detract from your knuckles.

But it isn't just your finger size that has to be taken into account. Your entire hand needs to be considered. The general rule is if you have small hands, keep the overall proportion of any ring small too, so it doesn't overwhelm your hand. If your hands are larger (or longer) you can carry off more elaborate, chunky styles—if that suits your personality. It's no use purchasing an attention-grabbing ring if you'll be uncomfortable with the attention or if it will draw attention to the wrong thing!

Chapter 13

GROOMING

> There must be quite a few things a hot bath
> won't cure, but I don't know many of them.

> —Sylvia Plath

Grooming sounds like such an old-fashioned concept, but sometimes it's okay to be old-fashioned! What exactly constitutes grooming? The dictionary definition of grooming is this: "(adjective) having the hair, skin, etc. well cared for; well-dressed, clean, and neat." I believe personal grooming also includes everything that makes you more attractive to be around, including attitude, posture, manners, and conversational skills. The reason I wanted to write specifically about grooming is it seems to be a neglected area nowadays, perhaps because it sometimes touches on embarrassing topics like body odor, bad breath, and excess hair. But if we're talking about *Grace in Your Second Act,* good grooming is essential.

Personal grooming is important because it's often the first impression someone has of you, and of course, you want that first impression to be positive. According to research conducted at the University of California, Los Angeles, upon meeting someone for the first time, we form an opinion of them within the first thirty seconds.

Cleanliness

The most basic element of good grooming is cleanliness. You would be surprised at how many people do not have adequate hygiene habits! And smelling bad is a real turnoff. Basically, everyone should shower every day and use deodorant. Then we need to take a look at perfume. Smelling good doesn't mean you have to empty an entire bottle of perfume over yourself! As we age, our sense of smell diminishes, so we need to make sure we don't overpower others because we've used far too much fragrance. It's also worth checking out lighter scents, which might suit you better. It's not necessary to wear perfume as long as you are clean. As a matter of fact, some people are allergic to it. Many body lotions have pleasant scents.

I believe a woman should smell like a woman and a man like a man! I'm not a big fan of strong fragrances for men or women. As a matter of fact, I prefer a man to smell freshly bathed, but scents are truly a matter of personal preference. A woman's fragrance should be subtle and feminine and fit the personality of the woman wearing it. I've been told many times that I smell good, but because I have been wearing the same fragrance for years, I can't smell it. If you choose, you can have a lighter fragrance for day and a little heavier one for evening. I choose to wear the same fragrance all the time. I used to wear a lighter one in the summer and a little heavier scent in the winter, but now I wear the same fragrance (Boucheron) all year-round. By the way, don't wear a fragrance just because it smells good on someone else. Wear what works best for your body chemistry. Friends of mine have tried Boucheron, and it smelled completely different on them and probably wasn't quite what they wanted.

Breath

Speaking of smelling good, no one wants to be near a person with bad breath.

Some of the most neglected parts of the body are the gums and teeth. A lot of people don't recognize the importance of proper brushing and flossing. Not doing so can affect the health of the whole body because bacteria can get in the bloodstream.

Bad breath can be caused by tooth decay, an abscess, or even stomach problems. A mint will not cover up the odor resulting from these conditions. Have a complete dental checkup at least once a year and your teeth professionally cleaned as often as your dentist recommends. I have my teeth cleaned by a dental hygienist every four months.

Use floss, whitening toothpaste, and white strips for a movie star sparkle.

And don't forget to brush your tongue. The tongue is covered with bacteria that mouthwash or drinking water doesn't get rid of. This can lead to bad breath or even tooth decay. Haven't you ever wondered why the doctor almost always says, "Stick out your tongue"? Red or white patches on the tongue can be a sign of diabetes, a bright pink tongue could be a sign of iron or vitamin B12 deficiency, and there are other things a doctor can tell about your health by looking at your tongue! Also, anxiety can lead to a dry mouth and/or tongue. If you have any of these symptoms, have your tongue checked by your doctor. Don't overbrush the tongue. You don't want to break the skin. There are also tongue scrapers that can do a good job of cleaning the tongue. Just by scraping, you are actually stimulating and massaging various internal areas of the body, much like acupuncture or acupressure.

Hydrating regularly is also a way to avoid bad breath. Dehydration reduces your saliva production, and saliva has antibacterial and antifungal properties that keep your mouth healthy and your breath smelling good.

And keep mouthwash handy!

Skin and Makeup

Cakey makeup is a definite no-no for the well-groomed woman. Apply makeup in natural light if possible. If you can't do that, ensure you have good lighting in the bathroom. Remember the light from a bulb is often a different shade from that of natural light, so it might give you a false reflection of how you really look.

Clumpy mascara is another makeup mistake. It's such a shame to see a woman with beautiful long lashes that are a clumpy, spidery mess. Just remember that most mascara thickens in time, so make sure you replace your mascara every six months, at least. And don't wear dressy, sparkly makeup during the day.

Clothes

Dress appropriately. If you're in a professional environment, don't reveal too much cleavage or leg (and certainly no belly should see an office or board meeting). Keep jewelry to a minimum too.

Nails

Nails and hands should be clean at all times. Neatly manicured nails with a neutral polish always look good. And long, gaudily painted talons are not generally appropriate for an everyday work environment.

Unwanted Hair

Those nasty stray hairs! Yes, ladies, we all have them. So let's make sure we get rid of them! Whether it's on your face or your body, it's never a pleasant sight. Remember if you can see it, so can everyone else.

Make sure your eyebrows are well shaped. Bushy, unkempt, salt-and-pepper eyebrows are very unattractive and aging. Groomed brows are beautiful. If you've neglected your brows, have them plucked professionally the first time. That will give you the best shape to work with. Color in the gray with brow pencil or a little hair dye if you need to.

Have your upper lip waxed regularly if you have a lady mustache. Maintaining a clear upper lip is easily done at home with waxing strips.

And of course, underarm, leg, and bikini hair should be removed if you're going to expose those parts to the world!

Hair

Whatever style you choose, make sure your hair is always clean and shiny. Depending on your hair type, long hair can sometimes be the easiest as you can always tie it back in a neat ponytail, giving you an instant well-groomed appearance.

Feet

Hot and sweaty feet have no place in the world of the well-groomed. For instantly fresh feet, spray your soles with chilled cologne, or try using refreshing chilled herbal water; peppermint or rose smell lovely without being overpowering. Make your own by adding a couple of drops of the essential oils to a spray bottle of water and storing it in the fridge. There are also powders and sprays made especially for the feet.

Shoes

Footwear tells a lot about a person. Make sure your shoes are always clean and well maintained. If you have some good leather shoes or boots, it's really worth the effort to give them a good old-fashioned shoeshine regularly. It will keep the leather supple, and they'll last longer and look fantastic.

Etiquette

Etiquette is another old-fashioned concept, but we can still keep up our standards even though many people choose to ignore the niceties! Be courteous. "Please," "Thank you," "Excuse me," and "I'm sorry" seem to be words that are on the decline, but I prefer to use them often. Being polite costs nothing but reflects well on you and is usually appreciated by the recipient. Carry yourself with grace. Presenting yourself well is a large part of successful grooming and allows you to project the best version of yourself. And remember manners when you're eating. Don't eat too fast or speak with your mouth full. All those lessons our mothers and grandmothers taught us are still relevant today! And never talk on your cell phone at the table. Turn it off.

Posture

Slouching isn't just unattractive; it's also aging. Pay attention to how you sit and stand. Pull those shoulders back. Your clothes will hang better, and you'll look younger and fitter.

Personal Grooming Kit for Your Purse

Try to carry a small makeup kit for touching up and maintaining your well-groomed appearance. As well as cosmetics, include a small packet of makeup remover pads, a nail file, and tweezers. (Yes, those stray hairs can appear at the most awkward times!)

Being well-groomed isn't just about what other people think of you; it's also how you feel about yourself. Not having to worry about smelling unpleasant, bad breath, stray hairs, etc. allows you to concentrate on being the best version of yourself. It will reduce anxiety, boost your self-confidence, and make a positive statement about who you are as a person. Remember you never get a second chance to make a first impression.

Chapter 14

DIET

What we have is "sickness" care.

—Maggie Kuhn

Webster's dictionary gives several definitions for the word *diet*. Most people focus on "to cause or choose to eat less." I prefer "the food and drink regularly consumed." I like to look at diet as a way of eating, not just eating to lose weight. After all, some people need a diet to gain weight. But no matter where you are on the scales, it's important to remember that diet plays a key role in how we age. I'm five feet, two, and prefer to weigh 120 pounds. I'm always working on those last five pounds, but I like a little meat on my bones so I'm not fanatical.

Back in the 1960s, when The 5th Dimension was just beginning, we had an arranger, Rene de Knight, in his fifties, who we, in our twenties, considered an older man. We labeled Rene a "health nut!" He did strange things like stand on his head and eat health food! Despite these idiosyncrasies, Rene traveled with the group and never got sick. Then I began to wonder, *Was that despite his odd habits, or because of them?* Well, due to Rene's influence, I became the "health nut" in the group. I developed an interest in juicing, diet, exercise, and anything that affected the body's health. Losing weight wasn't an issue (I was a size 2–4), and I rarely even got a cold, but I just wanted to feel my absolute best and ensure I had as much energy as possible without taking drugs, which were all around me. For a couple of years, I even became a vegetarian but found it a difficult challenge while traveling so frequently. It is much easier now that so many people are aware of the health benefits, and there are wonderful vegetarian and vegan restaurants across the country that serve very tasty food.

I won't prescribe a diet for health, weight gain, or loss because everybody is different and everyone has need of varying amounts of vitamins and supplements. And while I do much research and am quite knowledgeable, I do not consider myself an expert on the subject. I do know that one of the problems with so many of the fad diets is that they are usually too extreme, and while people do lose weight, when they begin to eat normally again; they often gain the weight they lost—plus some. I've seen this happen with friends and relatives. I admit I've been guilty of crash dieting too. When I wanted to lose a few pounds to get into a particular dress, I've eliminated everything white from my diet and cut out all complex carbohydrates for a week. This really isn't too different from how I normally eat and works without me gaining a lot of excess weight when I return to my more regular diet. Of course, there are sensible diet programs, such as Weight Watchers, that many people have used successfully. There are also good, informative health shows, such as *The Dr. Oz Show* on television, and lots of sites on the internet that have information about eating well. To remain in good health while losing or gaining weight, I suggest eating a sensible rather than faddy diet and, of course, exercising regularly. Come on. We all know this! It just takes discipline and determination to *do* it!

My diet is pretty simple and works for my personal lifestyle. When I'm home, I begin the day with a mug of room temperature or warm water with the juice of half a lemon. This is an old remedy I learned from my grandmother, and it really does cleanse the system.

After my prayer time, I then drink a protein drink before I walk. This drink usually consists of one scoop of protein powder (I prefer the vanilla crème flavor) in eight ounces of almond milk. Sometimes I use Trader Joe's organic reduced fat milk. To this I will add half a banana, about a tablespoon or two of peanut butter, and several shakes of cinnamon. I mix it in my NutriBullet blender. It's really quite tasty and gives me fuel for my walk.

After my walk (usually three miles around the lake in a park near my home), I have a hearty breakfast. I'm a grazer, which means I can't eat a lot at one sitting, so what seems hearty to me may not be so for you. Anyway, breakfast usually consist of gluten-free, steel-cut oatmeal with a pat of organic butter and organic walnuts, a dash of cinnamon, and a little Trader Joe's grade A maple syrup. Or for a change, I may have an organic free-range egg over easy, an Applegate brand organic chicken and apple sausage, and some fresh, organic blueberries with organic light whipped cream. Occasionally, I may have a sausage and a large salad for breakfast. By the way, breakfast does not have to consist of breakfast food. I've been known to eat some delicious leftover collard greens for breakfast.

I try to eat my largest meal at lunch. It usually consists of a large salad and gluten-free crackers or flatbread and some protein, like a piece of fish or chicken. To satisfy my sweet tooth, I may have a piece of fresh or dried fruit.

If I've eaten a salad for lunch, I may still have a salad for dinner. I just change or add to the ingredients to make it interesting. Again, I have a piece of fish or free-range chicken sautéed in olive oil for protein. Occasionally, I will have a small piece of grass-fed sirloin steak. At one time, I ate only vegetables, fruit, and a little chicken or fish. Then my doctor suggested that I eat some red meat occasionally, because he felt I need the protein from animal meat. I know that there are those who are very active like I and are vegetarians, but I must admit I do feel much better when I eat a little red meat.

You may have noticed that I do not necessarily follow the recommended formula for eating, which says, "Eat breakfast like a king, lunch like a prince, and dinner like a pauper!" I do believe this is a great idea and try to follow it, but usually my schedule is more suited to having my largest meal at lunch. This gives me a chance to take a break from work and gear up for the rest of the day. Also, I sometimes have business meetings at nice restaurants at lunchtime so I want to enjoy the moment. But take care ordering in restaurants. You don't always have to order a salad, some of which can be incredibly high in calories. For example, a Chinese chicken salad can have as many as 1200 calories, while a Big Mac has 550! I'm not suggesting you order a Big Mac, but try a thin-crust pizza, flatbread, or fish. And check the calories in those coffees. You can ruin an entire day's diet with just one purchase in Starbucks. A loaded Frappuccino can have as many as five hundred calories. That's another Big Mac you've just eaten!

Between meals, I will eat a piece of fruit or a slice of gluten-free bread with crunchy peanut butter and natural blueberry preserves. Being a grazer, I like to munch all day, so I try to eat healthy snacks like fruit or nuts. I stay away from sugary sodas (I have the occasional ginger ale) and eat fruit rather than drink calorie-laden fruit juice. You may have noticed I have some protein at each meal. I don't have any eating regimen written in stone, so if you spot me eating an occasional Haagen-Dazs ice cream, don't be surprised. It used to be my favorite guilty pleasure, but I am proud to announce that I have disciplined myself and have not had any for over a year. And surprisingly, I don't miss it. My favorite snack now is Element brand organic dipped rice cakes from Whole Foods. (I prefer the vanilla-orange flavor and try to limit my intake to the weekends.) I believe we have to be flexible and if we have an occasional treat, we won't feel limited as long as occasional doesn't happen too often! Be sure to get advice from your doctor before beginning any extreme change of eating or exercising habits. And remember you *can* be too thin!

We all have our own particular weaknesses. I recently conquered a sweet tooth and am still battling to drink more water. Again, this is something we all know, but to make it work, we must *do* it. I remember once a very much overweight woman asked me, "Girl, how do you stay so thin?" as she consumed her double-dip ice cream cone! This really happened. But I don't judge anyone. I used to eat a pint of rum raisin ice cream *with* pretzels at one sitting and not gain an ounce. Unfortunately, I can't do that now. What I didn't realize was that, even though I didn't gain weight—I was very physically active—I was still putting too much sugar in my body. Too much sugar contributes not only to diabetes but to Alzheimer's, cancer, and many other illnesses and attacks collagen and elastin, the two key ingredients to keeping your skin young. It takes a long time for your body to rid itself of sugar, and there is hidden sugar in so many processed foods, including vegetables.

As I've already said, diet isn't just about losing weight. It's really about a way of eating, and I want to talk about the best foods to eat to keep you and your body in the best possible condition. As the father of Western medicine, the ancient Greek physician Hippocrates said, "Let food be thy medicine, and medicine be thy food."

Most dieticians agree that what you eat makes a tremendous difference to how you age. The worst foods for aging are candies, fried bacon, donuts, flame-grilled burgers, sugary soft drinks, alcohol, and chips.

Your skin, joints, bones, and internal organs all need nourishment in order to stay in good condition. So I've compiled a top-twenty list of the essential foods that will help you look and feel great, followed by some simple recipes incorporating some of these health-giving ingredients.

1. Strawberries are rich in vitamin C and filled with collagen-protecting antioxidants, which help prevent aging.
2. Avocados are rich in vitamin E and monounsaturated fats, making them a great addition to your diet. They're really a delicious and valuable quick meal, drizzled with a little avocado or olive oil and sprinkled with some crunchy sea salt.
3. Blackcurrants. These too have lots of vitamin C as well as anthocyanins, which help protect collagen in the skin.
4. Cucumbers contain silica, which has been called "the beauty supplement" because it strengthens connective tissues and helps prevent sagging. And of course, the high water content provides great hydration.
5. Tomatoes contain lycopene, a powerful antioxidant that reduces the signs of aging and the risk of heart disease. Whether you eat them fresh in a salad or cooked in a pasta sauce, they're a tasty, adaptable, and healthy addition to any diet.
6. Salmon (and other fatty fish like mackerel, sardines, and tuna) is chock-full of omega-3 fatty acids, which have excellent antiaging properties for your skin, help curb inflammation of your joints, and have heart-healthy benefits.
7. Almonds contain lots of vitamins and minerals that are crucial to heart health and can help reduce cholesterol levels. But remember that while almonds are rich in nutrients, they're also high in calories. A few go a long way!
8. Walnuts are not only a really good source of many nutrients that contribute toward healthy skin, but they also help prevent joint inflammation and are a rich source of fiber.
9. Dark chocolate is actually good for us—in moderation! It's chock-full of antioxidants, which can help boost heart health. But like almonds, overindulging can lead to unwanted weight gain. Indulge

(just for your health, of course). Make sure it's just a tiny piece and that it has a cocoa content of at least 70 percent.

10. Olive oil is a staple in the heart healthy Mediterranean diet. It's packed with antioxidants, which can relieve inflammation and decrease the risk of chronic heart disease.

11. Garlic has for centuries been used as a natural remedy to treat a variety of ailments. In recent years, research has confirmed its potent medicinal properties and found that garlic can even help improve heart health by reducing blood pressure and cholesterol as well as possibly inhibiting blood clot formation.

12. Red bell peppers contain plenty of beta-carotene and vitamin C, both of which are important antioxidants for the skin.

13. Spinach and kale are rich in vitamins C and K as well as calcium, making them a good food for bone, joint, and heart health.

14. Broccoli is a good source of zinc, vitamin C and other vitamins, and lutein, which is good for healthy skin.

15. Oatmeal and other whole grains like brown rice, rye, barley, buckwheat, and quinoa are beneficial for a healthy heart.

16. Sweet potato contains magnesium and potassium, which help keep bones healthy.

17. Figs—both fresh and dried—contain high levels of calcium, potassium, and magnesium, which are all bone-strengthening nutrients.

18. Prunes (or dried plums) are a good, healthy, bone-density boosting snack.

19. Seeds (including flaxseeds and chia seeds) are good for a healthy heart. And what can be tastier than toasted sunflower seeds in a salad?

20. Legumes such as lentils and beans like garbanzos, kidney, pinto, and black are all healthy, fiber-rich foods that keep our bowels healthy and help lower cholesterol levels.

As you can see, what you put on your plate can influence just about every aspect of your health and appearance, from your skin to your heart.

While you're revamping your eating habits, you might enjoy an extra challenge: create a wellness garden for yourself. You don't necessarily need a backyard; a windowsill or balcony is just fine. Depending on the space available, you can grow an entire salad and enjoy the pleasure of enhancing your diet with your very own lettuces, tomatoes, and peppers. If space is limited, a simple herb garden is so satisfying. Basil, mint, rosemary, and oregano are perfect items to grow on your window ledge. There's nothing better than fresh basil in tomato salad, a refreshing cup of mint tea, and the addition of rosemary or oregano with your protein or vegetables.

And one other tip: Try not to eat while distracted. Don't watch TV or keep checking your phone. Sit at a table and savor every mouthful. You'll feel much more satisfied afterward. How many times have we all watched our favorite program and gobbled down a sandwich, then been surprised that the food has disappeared and we barely remember eating it?

In order to show you just how easy it is to eat healthy and well, I've included a few simple recipes that will satisfy your taste buds and give your general health a boost.

Recipes

The recipes I've included here could make up a complete meal—salad, main course, and dessert—if you're entertaining or just having a romantic dinner with your loved one. Alternatively, the salad and any of the "Trio of Tomato" dishes are good, standalone meals. I've also added a recipe for the ultimate minestrone, which is more of a stoup than a soup. It lasts for days and is so comforting on a cold winter's day. All the dishes contain ingredients that provide a healthy, balanced diet.

Florence LaRue's Easy Main Course Salad

(serves two or an appetizer salad for four)

Ingredients

1 romaine lettuce or mixed green of your choice
½ avocado
½–1 whole tomato
½ Persian cucumber

(You can actually use any vegetables like peppers, kale, celery, endive, shaved Brussels sprouts, etc., but these are the ones I prefer.)

1 one-oz. package of omega nut mix from Trader Joe's (or 1 oz. of nuts of your choice)

Method

Chop and mix vegetables in a large bowl and toss with salad dressing (preferably Florence LaRue's oil and vinegar). Do not use too much, as salad will be soggy!

Sprinkle nuts over and serve.

(For main course salad, add one protein: one organic chicken breast or thigh, a hard-boiled egg, fish of your choice, or grass-fed beef. Season chicken with "spike" seasoning and black pepper, sauté in olive oil, and set aside to cool.)

Florence LaRue's Oil and Vinegar Dressing

Ingredients
¾ cup extra-virgin olive oil
¼ cup seasoned vinegar
2 tablespoons Montreal chicken seasoning

Method
Mix all ingredients in a shaker; adjust to taste. (I don't measure!)

This dressing does not have to be refrigerated. (It will become solid). I've kept it in the cupboard for a week or more.

A Trio of Tomatoes

Cherry tomatoes look great and are deliciously sweet and full of flavor. They are just about the most versatile fresh ingredient you could have in your kitchen.

Just to prove my point, here are three separate dishes, all using the same basic ingredients and method. The core recipe is for roasted cherry tomatoes. With the addition of chopped basil and Parmesan cheese, this is a delicious sauce for pasta. Now let's make a couple of minor changes, and we have two fantastic and elegant dinner party dishes. For the first, we take the basic recipe, substitute some different flavorings, and add some salmon fillets, and we have created a colorful and flavorsome fish dish. For the third recipe, again, we take our basic recipe for roasted tomatoes, add some red pepper flakes and marjoram, pour the whole lot on top of some boneless, skinless chicken breasts, and—presto!—another dish is born. These three recipes are suitable for just about any meal, from an informal pasta supper to the most sophisticated dinner.

Roasted Cherry Tomatoes

(serves six)

Ingredients

2 tablespoons olive oil
24 oz. cherry tomatoes
1 teaspoon salt
1 teaspoon ground black pepper
¼ cup chopped flat-leaf parsley
¼ cup freshly grated Parmesan

Method

Preheat oven to four hundred degrees. Mix tomatoes, oil, salt, and pepper, and pour into a broiler-proof ceramic baking dish. Top with parsley and cheese. Bake tomatoes for ten minutes, then put under preheated broiler for about two minutes until the tomatoes begin to split and the cheese becomes golden. Serve over pasta.

Salmon with Roasted Tomatoes

(serves four)

Ingredients

Same as above. Omit parsley and cheese, but add the following:

3 teaspoons freshly chopped thyme
3 cloves garlic, chopped
4 salmon fillets
4 tablespoons fresh lemon juice

Directions

Mix tomatoes, oil, salt, pepper, thyme, and chopped garlic and bake as above, this time for fifteen minutes. Add fish to pan and bake for a further ten minutes, or until the fish flakes easily when tested. Serve fish on the bed of tomatoes. Drizzle with lemon juice.

Smothered Chicken

(serves four)

Ingredients

Same as roasted cherry tomatoes. Omit parsley and cheese, but add the following:

5 cloves garlic, chopped
1 ¼ teaspoon dried, crushed red pepper
2 tablespoons chopped, fresh marjoram (use oregano if you prefer)
4 skinless, boneless chicken fillets

Directions

Preheat oven to 450 degrees. Mix tomatoes, olive oil, garlic, red pepper, and one tablespoon marjoram. Place chicken in rimmed baking pan. Pour tomato mixture over, making sure chicken is well covered. Sprinkle with salt and pepper. Roast until chicken is cooked through and tomatoes are blistered, about thirty-five to forty minutes. Serve chicken covered with the tomatoes. Sprinkle with remaining marjoram.

Minestrone Soup

(serves fourish, but this is all very flexible!)

Ingredients

4 tablespoons olive oil
3/4 cup chopped onion
1/4 cup chopped celery
1/2 cup chopped carrots
1 (19-oz.) can cannellini beans
1/2 cup shredded cabbage, kale, or spinach

1 (14.5-oz.) can stewed tomatoes
1 tablespoon tomato paste
1 1/2 cups cubed potatoes
1 quart chicken broth
2 cloves garlic, minced
2 tablespoons dried parsley
1 teaspoon salt
1/2 cup elbow macaroni, cooked according to packet instructions (but make sure it's al dente)
1/2 cup grated Parmesan cheese

Directions

Heat olive oil in a heavy pot over medium heat. Add onion, celery, and carrots; sauté for a few minutes.

Add beans, tomatoes, tomato paste, potato, stock, garlic, parsley, and salt to the pot. Bring to a boil, cover, and reduce heat. Simmer for approximately one hour until vegetables are barely tender.

When soup is cooked, add cabbage (or spinach) and let it simmer for about thirty minutes so flavors mingle.

To serve, put a spoonful of cooked pasta at bottom of each bowl, then pour over the soup. Serve with grated Parmesan cheese on the side and a nice, warm, crusty baguette.

Red Fruit Salad

This is a supersimple dessert that looks great in a simple glass bowl. It incorporates many of the ideal fruits for good health.

All you have to do is mix together six ounces each of raspberries, blueberries, and blackberries. Add one cup of halved red grapes, two cups of watermelon (cubed), and three red plums (chopped). Dissolve two tablespoons of sugar into two cups of orange juice. Pour over the mixed fruits, and gently stir. Leave for at least one hour.

Chapter 15

FITNESS AND EXERCISE

Getting fit is a political act.
You are taking charge of your life.

—Jane Fonda

I have always been very physically active. Despite being five feet, two inches tall, when I was in junior high and high school, I played varsity basketball (I was fast and could jump high) and varsity field hockey and ran track. I also studied ballet and modern dancing and stayed on the dance floor at the school dances. Because of all this physical activity and a good metabolism, I could eat as much of anything I wanted and not gain an ounce.

As an adult, besides performing as a member of The 5th Dimension, I was a gym rat. I enjoyed exercising five to six days a week. (I've always considered Sunday as God's day and rested.) I even exercised before performing. It got my blood flowing. I used to do some kind of exercise for at least one hour on Monday, Wednesday, and Friday. This would consist of stretches, cardio, and weight exercises. On these days, I focused on arm and abdominal exercises. On Tuesday, Thursday, and Saturday, I walked for at least one hour (usually more) and focused on leg exercises. On nice days, I preferred to walk outside and up hills. If the weather didn't permit this, I walked on my treadmill. I used to enjoy playing tennis and participated in several celebrity tennis tournaments. Now, however, there are more golf tournaments, and I don't golf!

I began walking marathons in my sixties and have completed seven half marathons (13.3 miles each). I began training for them with the American Heart Association in 2009. Usually, when one is in a group, relationships are formed with just a few people. Well, I gravitated toward two ladies who became dear friends: Rosemary Kent and Marie Plumtree (who since married and is now Maria Stephens). We were nicknamed "the Three Fannies." Hey, we walked so fast, that's all you could see! In 2010, we received the California Dreamin' Racing series medal, which was awarded if one finished three California marathons in one year. We completed the Disney, Surf City, and Agoura Hills half marathons.

When I walked my first half marathon, I took much too much food—protein bars, fruit, nuts, "electrolyte jellybeans," etc.—for fear that I would run out of energy. Later, I realized most of that was not necessary, so I just carried a cut-up orange, a few nuts, and raisins.

I continue to exercise when I am traveling. Most hotels have a gym or there is a gym nearby. If not, I just walk in a park or along the street. I sometimes walk up and down the stairs in the hotel several times for cardio exercise.

As the title of this chapter indicates, it's not just about exercise but fitness too. We can't prevent death, but we can prevent "preventable death!" How do we do that? It's actually very simple. The main causes of preventable death are smoking, drinking excessively, and obesity. Of course, there are many more subdivisions. (To avoid obesity, we have to eat well, which means being aware of our sodium and fat intake and limiting sugar. These are all subjects I deal with in the chapter about diet.) But basically, these are the most preventable causes of sickness.

I like to have an adjustment by a chiropractor once a month. This is especially good for me because I often take long flights. After I gave birth to my son, I performed in Japan and slept in a comfortable but soft bed. When I returned to the States, my lower back hurt so badly that I had to be carried into my chiropractor's office. Because I am very active, chiropractic adjustments are not a luxury but a necessity!

Chiropractic adjustments are also good for people who sit at a desk for extended lengths of time. But don't just go to anyone you see advertising locally. It's important to do some research and/or get a reference to find a qualified chiropractor.

Posture

There is an old Asian saying that is translated, "The condition of the spine determines one's age." In other words, the healthier your spine, the better your posture, the younger you are. Or at least the younger you appear to be. But beyond appearance, poor posture can also affect the internal organs and cause lower back pain among other ailments. Good posture is, therefore, an important element of aging with grace. It can also make one appear to be five to ten pounds lighter, which is no bad thing! I wonder if my mother knew more about posture than I realized, because she would always tell me, "Stand (or sit) up straight." Because I was a shy, late bloomer, I was embarrassed when I developed breasts and would slump to try to take attention off my chest! Even now, I constantly have to remind myself to stand and sit up straight.

Yoga, Pilates, and swimming are all good ways to strengthen your core muscles, which in turn addresses muscle imbalances that lead to poor posture.

To summarize, aging well is about quality of life. We all want to be able to enjoy every minute possible. And that means keeping in shape and being able to do all the things we want to do. If you look at people in their twenties and thirties, it's very hard to differentiate between those who exercise and those who don't. But if you check out people over sixty, it's pretty easy to see who's been working out regularly.

Here are a few suggestions to help you enjoy every minute of this wonderful, blessed life.

Getting Started

The most important thing about exercising is that it shouldn't be a chore. If you don't enjoy it, you won't do it! Find something you really like so you'll look forward to it. Arrange your daily schedule to include exercise, but be flexible. Be disciplined, but don't be hard on yourself. If your work or family commitments don't allow you to exercise one day, that's okay. Just try to sneak in a little stretching or fast walking as you go about your chores, but do be as consistent as possible.

If you haven't exercised for years (or ever) you need to start slowly. You don't want to injure yourself because you'll just be discouraged and give up. Who needs pain when you can have fun? Create achievable milestones and work toward them. If you've never worked with weights, start light and increase as you get stronger. If you've never gone on long walks, start with a distance you can manage comfortably then go a little further each week. Another good way to start gently is to just do a little bit more of what you already manage, such as taking a longer walk to the store or walking up escalators at a train station, airport, or hotel.

Keep Moving

One of the most important things you can do for yourself is *move!* The reason for this is quite simple. Exercise helps you loosen up by stretching and strengthening stiff tissues as well as lubricating the joints. It also helps strengthen your bones. Surprisingly, bone loss actually begins around thirty, although it accelerates after menopause. As a rough guide, for each year after fifty, you lose an average of 0.5 percent bone. So it's never too early or too late to start exercising.

Bone loss may also be a side effect of certain medicines, such as thyroid medication and chemotherapy drugs, or may be a result of other illnesses. Your doctor may prescribe a supplement, depending on your bone density. Calcium, glucosamine with chondroitin, phosphorous, potassium, and vitamin D are some helpful supplements for bone strength. Be sure to check with your doctor, even if you take natural supplements to assure that you are taking the correct supplements and the correct dosages. For instance, although osteoporosis can be remedied by taking calcium supplements, it depends on the way the calcium is absorbed and used by the body and the *type* of calcium taken is important. For these reasons alone, I cannot stress too much the importance of checking with your health care provider when taking any type of medicine or herbs for any ailment. I cannot recommend what I take to another person because everybody is different and has their own nutritional needs. I am blessed to have pretty strong bones, but my doctor did prescribe a low dose of calcium. I also eat cheese. I know it has a lot of calories, but I make up for it elsewhere, and when I do eat it, I try to eat raw cheese, although Trader Joe's Havarti is my favorite!

The key to fitness at any age is to find an activity you enjoy and, as I said, move! Even if you are unable to exercise vigorously, you can still walk or dance.

Walking

Of course, as I've matured, my regimen has changed. These days, my exercise program consists mostly of walking, but I don't do marathons anymore. I usually walk three miles a day around a lake near my home, starting early in the morning before the air has been polluted with exhaust from cars (and before I get busy doing other things). Walking also helps to prevent osteoporosis. It is a weight-bearing exercise, which increases bone density by depositing more mineral to the bones, especially those of the legs, spine, and hips. I also try to walk fast for a short period to get the heart rate up for maximum benefit. Speed walking is great exercise to help toward weight loss goals. And in case you're still in any doubt about the benefits of walking, a recent Cambridge University study showed that just twenty minutes a day may reduce your risk of premature death by 16–30 percent!

Walking also gives me an opportunity to appreciate God's wonderful creations. As I walk, I thank God for all the beautiful things I see—the flowers, trees, animals, etc.—and thank Him for the fact that I have my sight and health and live in a country where I am free to enjoy the simple things in life. Even as I am writing this, I am feeling such joy and energy and excitement about my blessings. I have stopped taking these things for granted.

Be sure to wear the proper clothing when walking, and don't forget a cap, sunglasses, and sunblock to protect you on sunny days (even dark-complexioned people), and a scarf on windy days. The biggest mistake I see people make is wearing the wrong shoes. They go out in all kinds of footwear, from flip flops to clogs. I can't stress enough how very important it is to be fitted with the correct walking shoes. Wearing improper shoes can cause all kinds of problems, including back or knee pain, which will ultimately discourage you from walking.

Take the time to stretch both before and after you walk, and stay hydrated. I always carry a small bottle of water with me. I like to eat a little protein for energy before walking, but not too much. Usually I have a protein drink: almond milk, protein powder, and frozen blueberries or a slice of gluten-free whole wheat toast with crunchy peanut butter and natural blueberry preserves.

If you decide walking is your way of moving, get motivated. Taking a dog for a walk (a neighbor's if you don't have one) is a good way of helping someone out. Also get a pedometer. You'll be surprised how much fun it is to push yourself to take those extra steps. Walk whenever you can—to the store, to work, to visit friends, etc. If you can't walk all the way, try going part of the way and parking your car a little distance from your destination.

It's also a fantastic way to explore your town. You'll be amazed at the beautiful places or funky shops you'll discover when you're on foot.

If you're on the phone, pace, don't sit. If you have a friend who's always a thirty-minute phone call, start walking at the beginning of the phone call.

Get into the Pool

Swimming is also an excellent way to exercise because you need to move your whole body against the resistance of the water. It's a good all-round activity because it keeps your heart rate up but takes some of the impact stress off your body while building endurance, muscle strength, and cardiovascular fitness. Ideally, you should aim to build your active swim time to twenty minutes, three times a week. But like every other exercise, start slowly and increase your time and distance as you grow stronger. Don't overdo it! And if you don't swim, try exercising in the shallow end of the pool or take a class. Most recreation centers have classes for all abilities, even nonswimmers.

Water exercise is great for the elderly who are having physical problems that prevent them from going to a gym. I know of an older gentleman who does well with water exercise classes to ease his arthritis but can hardly walk on dry land. As a matter of fact, I was instructed to exercise in the shallow end of the pool when I was recovering from arthroscopic knee surgery to repair a torn meniscus.

Yoga

As we get older, we all lose muscle strength and flexibility. Our balance also isn't as good as it once was due to loss of muscle strength and joint flexibility, as well as reduced vision and reaction time. Additionally, the risk of inner ear dysfunction increases as we age, which can cause unsteadiness. So we have to ensure we make up for what we lose. *Yoga* is a group of physical, mental, and spiritual practices or disciplines that gently and effectively address most of these issues.

I suggest you try out a class nearby and learn from a professional. You can also find some very good tutorials online.

Weight Lifting

Weight lifting contributes to good bone health. The golden rule, which I follow, is more repetitions with lighter weights. Not only is that a safer approach, but you can retain a soft, feminine look while building muscle strength. I advise you to go to a gym or seek the aid of a knowledgeable personal trainer before beginning a weight lifting regimen to avoid injuring yourself. Don't be hard on yourself if you gain a pound or two when you begin exercising. Muscle weighs more than fat. I once gained five pounds and lost a dress size!

You Don't Need a Gym!

Without thinking about it, most of us do some kind of workout as part of our daily living! Housework, such as cleaning sinks, vacuuming, and emptying the dishwasher, counts as physical activity. If you want to up the ante, put on some of your favorite music and dance while you work. Dusting, vacuuming, mopping, and scrubbing can become fun with the right beat! And if you need some inspiration, check out Robin Williams in *Mrs. Doubtfire!*

Parking farther away at the market and carrying shopping bags that extra distance, gardening, taking care of young children who need to be picked up and carried, or walking up and down the stairs a couple of times more than necessary are easy ways to move your body and burn a few extra calories.

Even watching television can give you a fitness boost. Instead of sitting on the sofa and munching cookies or potato chips, get on the floor and do a few crunches, leg lifts, or stretches while you're watching your favorite program.

Hula Hoop

When was the last time you picked up a hula hoop? You were probably around eleven or twelve. Well, I've got news for you. It's time to start hula hooping again! The American Council for Exercise found it burned four hundred calories per hour and is a great way to work the core muscles in your back and stomach. You can burn calories, improve your posture, and become a kid again!

In order to start, don't borrow a hoop from your children or grandchildren. You need a grown-up sized hoop. Once you've conquered (or remembered) the art of hula hooping, try getting a weighted hoop, which is designed specifically to give your body an extra workout.

And one other thought: While you're raiding your childhood toy closet, remember how much fun you had as a kid jumping rope? Well, you're never too old! Try getting a full-sized skipping rope. It's another fantastic way of burning calories and strengthening our legs, arms, and core.

Dance

Who doesn't love to dance? Dancing is a great cardio exercise that benefits your lungs and blood flow as well as helps bones stay strong. And the great thing about dancing is that it doesn't feel like exercise, so you might be more motivated to stick with it. There are so many different classes available, from Zumba to line dancing. Here's a list of some dance disciplines you might like to try:

- Ballroom. Whether you're waltzing, foxtrotting, or doing the quickstep, ballroom dancing helps to improve balance, heart, and lung function, and you have a partner you can hold on to!
- Latin. Tango, cha-cha, samba, rumba, paso doble, and jive are faster, more energetic forms of ballroom dancing. Not only are they great for strengthening bones and flexibility, but the more complicated moves help boost cognitive function.
- Salsa. Good for cardio and core because you have to pull in your stomach while dancing.
- Tap builds bone density.

- Ballet and contemporary dance improve muscle tone and boost the brain.
- Zumba burns calories (six hundred to one thousand calories in a one-hour class), tones your entire body, benefits your heart, and improves coordination.

Whichever type of dance class you choose, you can be guaranteed you'll come out destressed and smiling. They're also a great way to make new friends.

As I noted in the introduction, it is never too early or too late in life to start your journey toward being in your best health possible. The advice I would give to my grandchildren (or any other young person who will listen) is to prepare for your future by taking care of your health now. But for those of you who aren't so youthful, just start slowly, and listen to your body. If you have any questions at all, ask the advice of your doctor or health practitioner.

Chapter 16

SLEEP

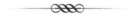

Dreams are illustrations—from the book your soul is writing about you.

—Marsha Norman

When people used to talk about the importance of "beauty sleep," they hit the nail right on the head. Sleep is one of the most underappreciated beauty and health aids. Proper sleep is important not only for beauty but for optimum health. Believe it or not, the amount of sleep you get even affects your diet, and getting a good night's sleep can help if you want to lose weight. If you don't get enough sleep, your body releases hormones that are directly related to your appetite. Additionally, as we all know, being tired increases our stress levels, often sending us to the fridge or cookie jar to make ourselves feel better. Good quality sleep also helps strengthen your immune system and boosts your energy. So as you can see, sleep is an extremely important part of good health, both short and long term.

Most doctors still adhere to the old adage that one should get seven to eight hours of sleep a night for optimum health. I believe that this varies for different people. I am well rested if I get six good hours of sleep. Unfortunately, I don't always sleep as well as I should, but I'm working on it. Here's a list of tips that should help you get a better night's rest, starting with creating the best environment:

- If possible, remove your computer and work items from your bedroom. That way, your brain recognizes it as being a calm, stress-free environment and strengthens the association between bed and sleep.
- Pay attention to the temperature in your bedroom. It should be comfortably cool, somewhere between sixty and sixty-seven degrees, depending on your personal preference.
- Your bedroom should be dark. Light at night disrupts your body's sleep cycle and suppresses the hormone melatonin, which induces sleep. Use blackout curtains if necessary, and turn the light from digital clocks away from the bed. Use a sleep mask if that helps.
- Your bedroom should be quiet. Do not go to sleep with the television on. It took me a long time to break this unhealthy habit. I still do it occasionally, but I find that I sleep better and am more rested when I turn the television off before going to sleep. By the way, this only happens when I fall asleep on the couch or I'm staying in a hotel. I decided not to have a television in my bedroom at home. If you live in a noisy area (or your spouse snores!), use earplugs.
- Make sure you have a comfortable mattress. The degree of softness or hardness is a very individual preference, but the mattress should support the body properly. An investment in a good mattress is an investment in good health.
- Sleep clothing, if you wear it, should be loose and comfortable.

Once you've created the perfect environment, prepare your body and your mind.

- Get regular exercise, but not within two to three hours of bedtime. If possible, exercise in the morning or before dinner.
- To avoid sleepless nights, try not to have any caffeine after 2:00 p.m.
- Do not eat less than two to three hours before going to bed.
- Begin to wind down during the last hour or so before you go to bed. Create a calming routine that separates your day from your sleep time. Indulge in a peaceful activity, such as reading, listening

to music, or taking a leisurely bath with soft lights and scented candles. Meditation or prayer are also effective ways of destressing before bed. For some people, using an electronic device, such as a laptop; can make it hard to fall asleep, because the particular type of light emanating from the screens of these devices is activating to the brain. Also, it's so tempting to check your emails, and before you know it, you're working! If you have trouble sleeping, it's definitely best to avoid screen time.

- Stick with a consistent bedtime. Of course, that's not always possible and it would be foolish to be rigid about this, but when you can, maintain a regular sleep schedule. That way, you begin to train your internal clock, which will help you fall asleep faster.
- Natural melatonin can also help you fall asleep. Try eating some walnuts, almonds, pineapple, bananas, or oranges. They all contain significant amounts of melatonin.
- Drink some warm milk. The benefit of warm milk making you sleepy isn't an old wives' tale. Milk contains tryptophan, which is sleep inducing. However, if you're not a milk drinker, some chamomile tea with a little honey is very soothing.
- A lavender-scented candle helps peaceful sleep.

If you still can't sleep, don't lie in bed awake. That in itself can be very stressful. If you're still wide-awake after twenty minutes, do something calming until you feel sleepy, like reading or listening to soft music. Personally, I like to get up and do something for about thirty minutes and then try to go to sleep again. I've been very productive in the wee hours of the night, because there are no phones ringing and it's quiet so I can focus on whatever project I am working on. But that may not work for everyone. For some people, that gets the brain stimulated and just keeps you awake. You have to know yourself!

Many people benefit from naps in the middle of the day. Studies show that in countries where siestas are practiced, people work more efficiently. I'm working on trying to take a nap after lunch, but I usually get so involved in projects that it is a difficult habit for me to form. If you are going to take a nap, don't do so after around 3:00 p.m. or it just might make it difficult for you to fall asleep later.

And one final thought about getting a healthy night's rest: Every night before you go to sleep, think of four things that you're grateful for. That's just good for your soul.

Chapter 17

STRESS

⊶⊷

God grant me the serenity to accept the things
I cannot change, the courage to change the things
I can, and the wisdom to know the difference.

—Reinhold Niebuhr

Stress and anger are the two big developers of wrinkles! It seems that these days, it's very hard to find one person who is not experiencing some kind of stress—be it with family, finances, or work. In case you need reminding, the definition of stress is a state of mental or emotional strain or tension resulting from adverse or very demanding circumstances. Well, we've all been there, haven't we? But here's the important thing to remember: We often choose to put importance on things we have no control over. And if we have no control over a situation, we have to learn to deal with it but not *stress* over it. It's so easy to talk about how to overcome stress, but it takes practice and determination to actually *do* it. The following are some suggestions:

Develop a friendship with someone with whom you can share your problems honestly. A shared load is easier to carry. But be sure it is someone who will not just gossip and share your private information with everyone. That will add to your stress rather than decrease it.

Don't refuse to give or accept help from others! Once I was driving a friend's car and, because it was much bigger than my car, had trouble parking it. A gentleman behind me angrily shouted, "Lady, can't you park that car?" I said, "No! Can you please help me!" He chuckled and parked the car for me. Now there could have been angry words shouted back and forth and both of us could have ended up very stressed. Instead, he felt like a hero, and I was helped. Learning how to handle unexpected situations really can help to avoid stress.

Take your cares to God, no matter what your religion. There are reasons the Bible states over and over, "Do not worry." Your body can heal itself of cuts and bruises, but stress can cause permanent damage. "It has been proven that a tranquil mind promotes good health" (Proverbs 14:30 New King James Version). God is so good.

You're reading this book in a country where there is freedom to achieve whatever you desire if you do as my mother told me: work hard and trust in God.

As for worrying, I believe the author Ruth Rendell said it best in *Talking to Strange Men.* "The best course was to buy a house across from a cemetery and look at it every morning. Reminding yourself where it all ended anyway, you'd never get upset about anything again."

When I need to destress, I turn to prayer. I read my Bible or inspirational books. And I love to walk, so sometimes if I'm really busy, I make my walk a prayer walk. Being with nature seems to calm me down. I remind myself that I'm grateful I can see, smell, and hear and grateful I can walk unassisted at my age. In fact, as much as being a prayer walk, it's also a gratitude walk. I thank the Lord when I look at the sky and for the ducks and geese I see when I walk around the lake near my home. I always say good morning to the people I meet on my way. Sometimes they're looking at the ground because they don't want to acknowledge anyone and, of course, I respect that choice. But most people eventually respond. They smile and say good morning. Sometimes, if I'm preoccupied, they're the first to say hello. A smile and a pleasant greeting cheer people up. Who knows? It might be the only agreeable thing that happens to them that day.

I'm also fortunate that I've been able to create a "stress-free zone" in my home. I call it my spiritual corner. It's a cozy corner of my bedroom in which I've placed items that are most important to me. The focal point is my grandma's chair, which I have had recovered in a pretty fabric. It's comfortable and I feel connected with her when I sit in it. I also have a Midnight Jasmine-scented candle nearby, together with my two favorite books—my Bible and *Jesus Calling*—which are filled with words of wisdom. (I also read a proverb every day. *Jesus Calling* was given to me by a very dear friend, so I treasure it.) I also have a prayer pillow and pictures of my loved ones. I say my prayers there every day. It's cozy, spiritual, and comfortable and creates a perfect sanctuary for me. I suggest you try to establish a similar stress-free zone for yourself. You don't need a lot of space, just a little imagination and a few simple items to create your oasis. Here are a few tips:

1. Make sure you have a comfortable chair or recliner and keep a nice, soft blanket beside it so you can snuggle up, cocoonlike, when the mood takes you.
2. Have some kind of surface nearby that will hold your special items. It can be a desk, nightstand, small table, or tray.
3. Next, carefully choose the meaningful objects you wish to surround yourself with. Don't clutter the area, or you'll just end up even more stressed! Select a few very special items that make your heart sing, like photos of loved ones, special books (just one or two), candles, flowers, perhaps a religious icon, a picture of a special place where you found peace and tranquility, or some personal sentimental treasures that make you smile when you look at them.

Try to keep that area specifically for that use so that no outside influences can intrude in your quiet time.

Now that you have your oasis of peace in your home, you're ready to explore other ways of reducing stress. It is important that you be yourself. If two people are identical, one of them is unnecessary! That's my way of reminding myself not to try to be everything to everybody; it's impossible. Be the best parent, friend, and partner you can, but make sure you have enough time for them *and* you.

A few other simple ways of keeping stress at bay are the following:

- If you're angry, think before you speak. Arguments can be exhausting and self-defeating. In order to avoid saying something in anger that you might later regret, write your grievances down in a letter expressing your feeling. Then tear it up! You will have vented without the stress of a heated confrontation.

- Negotiate. You don't always have to be right. Sometimes winning is meeting in the middle.

- Make time for relaxation and hobbies. Most of us have to work to feed, clothe, and house ourselves. But our souls and creativity need nourishing too.

- Arrive in plenty of time. Being late is, more often than not, a crisis of your own making. If you leave a few minutes earlier than you think you should, you'll avoid arriving at your destination flushed, out of breath, and with stratospheric stress levels.

- Spend time with friends and family who make you smile. Love and laughter will eliminate tension every time!

- Improve the quality of your sleep. (I discuss this in another chapter.)

- Don't wait for the perfect moment to do something. Chances are it will never arrive and you will have missed out on so much.

- Slow down. Okay, I know that's difficult, but do you really have to rush everywhere? Take time out from your busy schedule to notice what's going on around you.

- If you're feeling stressed, get moving. A brisk fifteen-minute walk will work off nervous energy and clear your head. And walking is a great way to, quite literally, stop and smell the roses!

- Hug your friends and loved ones. Physical contact with others is beneficial.

- As Monty Python fans will agree, it's important to "always look on the bright side of life!" If something is going on in your life that isn't what you'd hoped for or anticipated, try to reframe it as a teaching moment rather than a disaster. If you take an optimistic approach to problems, they sometimes seem easier to solve.

- Enjoy life when it's good. Remember today you didn't get stuck in traffic, you found the perfect parking space, that dress you loved was on sale, etc. Little victories count.

- Don't immerse yourself in politics and the news. Of course you should be aware of what's happening in the world, but life will go on whether you worry about what's going on in Washington or not!

- Don't spend too much time on social media. Remember friends on Facebook are rarely the friends who count!
- Be kind to others. Nothing makes you feel as good as making someone else's day better.
- If you're working and feeding a family, try planning meals a week ahead. Make your shopping list and buy everything you need in one trip. You'll save time and anxiety.
- Write down your worries in a notebook. Sometimes, writing things down help clear our minds.
- Turn a negative thought into a positive one. If you have a problem that really can't be resolved, or a situation that can't be changed, instead of saying, "I give up," say, "I accept. Now what can I do to make this situation better." And pray about it. Prayer works.
- Buy yourself *me* flowers.
- Don't stress about getting older. The alternative is much worse! Embrace who you are and how you look. Focus on leaving a positive legacy. Don't be too *me* oriented. Help someone else, even if it's just with an encouraging phone call.

Physical Reaction to Stress

As you probably know, the danger of stress isn't just about what's going on in our heads. It affects our bodies negatively. There is a direct correlation between stress and such conditions as high blood pressure, heart disease, and diabetes. Stress can also affect your weight and reduce your sex drive. None of that sounds attractive to me!

Originally, stress was all about fight or flight. That's all well and good when the danger is short term, like a wild animal or a fire we have to escape, but we're not built for the kind of long-term stress we put ourselves under in modern society. And this long-term stress can do long-term damage.

A lot of us have symptoms that occur whenever we're particularly anxious. It might be a rash, upset stomach, panic attack, etc. There are any number of ways our bodies react when we feel that life is out of control. The important thing to do is to recognize these symptoms, step back from our problems, and regain control of our lives, insofar as that's possible. If we feel we're in the driver's seat, our body will stop producing the fight or flight hormones.

If you are showing the physical signs of stress, here are a few tips to help alleviate them:

1. Make sure you have a healthy diet with plenty of fruit, vegetables, whole grains, and low-fat protein. Avoid sugar, salt, caffeine, and alcohol.
2. Get as much sleep as possible. Avoid watching TV late at night.
3. Exercise.
4. Relax by doing yoga, meditation, or simply deep breathing exercises.
5. Talk to your friends. I don't mean bore them to death with your problems, but talking about your feelings with someone you trust is a definite help.
6. Pray. Trust God.

Your Very Own Bill of Rights

As we've seen, a major source of stress is the feeling that your life is out of control. It's important to know that you have certain rights in any relationship, whether it's with family, friends, colleagues, or people whose paths cross with yours in general. I thought it might be helpful to finish this chapter with a personal "bill of rights"—a guideline to reasonable expectations in our day-to-day relationships. So remember the following:

1. You have the right to be treated with respect.
2. You have the right not to be responsible for anyone else's problems.
3. You have the right to be angry sometimes.
4. You have the right to say *no*.
5. You have the right to make mistakes.
6. You have the right to have your own teachings, opinions, and convictions.
7. You have the right to change your mind and decide on a different course of actions.
8. You have the right to negotiate for change.

9. You have the right to ask for emotional support or help.
10. You have the right to protest about any unfair treatment or criticism.

Eliminating all stress from our lives is an unrealistic goal. But we can *manage* stress. I hope that some of the tools I've given you in this chapter will help you to do just that.

Chapter 18

HOME SPA DAY

Life is too short not to treat yourself occasionally. A home spa day is a great way to feel and look good. The "perfect" day is a very personal thing. For me, I like to take a warm bath with Epsom salts and bubble bath, then have my masseuse come to my home and work the tension from my body. Then, I'll put on comfortable clothes, light a candle, listen to music, and take a long nap. Some people would prefer to spend hours in the bathroom, soaking in a perfumed bath and slathering lotions all over. Others still would just put on a face mask and watch their favorite movies. So on the basis that a luxurious day of pampering means very different things for different people, I've come up with a list of ways that you can spoil yourself at home. Just pick and choose the indulgences you prefer. Or, of course, you can try them all!

Preparation

This is a day to focus on *you*. Switch off your phone! Don't check your emails or do anything work related. Remember everyone deserves some time off.

As I've mentioned in other parts of this book, preparation is an essential element of reducing stress. And let's face it. The last thing you want on your home spa day is stress, so prepare everything you need in advance. Get all your lotions, potions, face masks, towels, music, candles, food, and drink ready. It's also a good idea to plan out a schedule. Then all you have to do is focus on yourself. You deserve it.

- Hydration is important every day, but on a spa day, take a little time to make it special. Fruit-infused water is delicious to sip all day long, and it looks pretty. Fill a large jug with water then add a few slices of lemon, orange, cucumber, strawberries, watermelon, kiwi, grapefruit, or mint leaves (which smell wonderful) and put it in the refrigerator. You can pour yourself some throughout the day. It gets better as the fruit flavor becomes more concentrated.
- Have some healthy snacks on hand, like hummus, cut-up vegetables, and avocados. Make a big bowl of fruit salad, using all your favorite fruits. Now you have a healthy, tasty snack you can pick at all day. If you like, you can put a dollop of Greek yogurt and a spoonful of honey on top of one of your servings.
- Slice cucumber for your eyes. Cucumber slices make a perfect eye mask. Put the slices in the fridge until you're ready to use them.

Prepare Your Bathroom
- The day before, make sure your bathroom is clean and uncluttered. It will be so much more relaxing and spa-like.
- Put some flowers or a pretty green plant in the bathroom.
- Get a bath pillow. It makes that long soak even more luxurious.
- Light a scented candle or essential oil diffuser to give you that spa smell. Use a calming smell like lavender, vanilla, cinnamon, or jasmine.
- Dim the lights, if possible. If not, light a few extra candles so you can turn the lights off when you sink into the tub.
- Have a cozy robe, fresh towels, and clean washcloths ready.
- Bring in a glass of your infused water. You'll want to keep hydrated while you're soaking.

Prepare Yourself
- Just in case you didn't get the message the first time, turn off that phone!
- Do some gently stretches, like cow and cat. Nothing strenuous. You can take a day off from your crunches and squats.

- Apply a hair mask that best suits your hair type. Alternatively, massage coconut oil into dry hair. Comb it through, then put on a shower cap. This will enable your own body heat to "bake" the oil into your hair, giving it a really intense treatment.
- Remove any makeup with a gentle cleanser.
- Steam your face over a bowl or sink of hot water to open up your pores.
- Gently exfoliate your skin.

Bath

A bath is an essential part of a spa day. The warm water will soothe your muscles and relax you for the afternoon nap or long night's sleep you'll enjoy after your pampering session.

- Take a cleansing shower first.
- Run a warm but not too hot bath. You don't need any expensive bath products to create the perfect experience. Epsom salt works as well as any of them. You can use Epsom Soothing Lavender Bath Salt for Soaking if you'd like to add an aromatherapy element. Alternatively, you can pour some drops of your favorite essential oils into the water.
- Before you get into the tub, after you've cleansed your face, apply a face mask—whichever kind you prefer that suits your skin type. Sheet masks are particularly good as they're infused with excellent ingredients and eliminate the need to apply messy pastes.
- Turn down the lights, play some relaxing music, and climb into that gorgeous, fragrant bath. Apply the cold cucumber slices to your eyes.
- Close your eyes and enjoy the luxury of this special *me* time.
- After a nice long soak, it's time to exfoliate. Using a loofah or body mitt, gently scrub your body to get rid of those dead skin cells.
- Remove your face mask and gently massage the remaining product into your skin. It will absorb beautifully and leave your face feeling extra soft.

After Your Bath

- When you emerge from the bath, apply body lotion while your skin is still warm and damp. It will absorb much better. Remember to apply the lotion to elbows and feet as well as your legs, arms, and shoulders.
- Put on your soft robe or cozy pajamas.
- If you want, give yourself a manicure and pedicure. Now would be a great time because your nails will be soft from soaking in the tub. If you don't want to do that, give yourself a foot massage with some coconut oil and put on some soft socks. You can leave them on overnight. In the morning, your feet will be supersoft.

Spend the rest of the day or evening relaxing. Try to stay in pampering mode. You've indulged your body; now take care of your mind. Enjoy eating some of the delicious snacks you've prepared for yourself. Take your time and really taste the food. Try to avoid harsh lights, and play the soft music you were listening to in the bath.

When you're ready, curl up in your favorite chair or on the bed and relax some more. You can read a book you specially enjoy or watch TV. But avoid the news and action or horror movies. Treat yourself to your favorite chick flick or romantic comedy. A feel-good movie really will make you feel good!

If you don't want to read or watch TV, sit outside in your backyard or by your window and enjoy the view. Alternatively, this would be a perfect time to meditate.

Take time to wind down your day slowly. Perhaps have a cup of chamomile tea with honey. When you're ready for bed, brush your teeth slowly, thinking back over the peaceful day you've just spent—alone, happy, and content. Continue to think calming thoughts as you lie in bed.

If it's earlier in the day, try to take a power nap. Lie down with a soft blanket over you and a comfortable pillow under your head, play some relaxing music, and enjoy the way your body feels. You can put another couple of cucumber slices on your eyes to make them sparkle even more if you're going out later in the evening.

When you're preparing for your pampering day, make sure you have the following items in the house:

- ingredients for the infused water and snacks you'll be making for yourself
- a scented candle (I like Night Jasmine, but choose a scent that works for you.)
- a bath mitt for exfoliating (It will leave your skin feeling soft and smooth.)
- body scrub
- coconut oil
- face mask
- moisturizer
- Epsom salts
- any essential oils you might choose to use
- bubble bath

With the correct planning, you'll find just one day of pampering will make you feel as though you've just had a wonderful vacation—without the stress of airports and packing!

Chapter 19

WORK AND BEYOND

T he old-fashioned concept of retirement applies less and less these days. It used to be that some people would look ahead to retirement as the golden years when they could enjoy an easy life after years of toil in a job they didn't enjoy. For others, it was a depressing thought—endless years ahead with nothing to fill them, feeling useless and unfulfilled. But that's all changed now. Ironically, although ageism is rampant in our society, older people find themselves busier and more in demand than ever.

No matter what we've achieved professionally or personally, we have earned the comfort of no longer needing to prove ourselves. Our record stands for itself. If we enjoy our work, we can continue to pursue our chosen career. If it's less than satisfying and you can either retire or work part time, that's a decision worth considering. And then there's another option. Perhaps now is the time to change direction and work in an area you've always wanted to be in. But whichever path you choose—work, retirement, or career change—it doesn't mean you have to stop being active and productive. In fact, it just may be the right time to pursue your dreams.

Let's look at the options. When you're at the point when you want to look at your future journey and decide where you want to focus your efforts, ask yourself the following questions:

- What are your skills? Are you artistic? A great organizer? Do you love to cook?
- What's your motivation? Do you want to earn money, meet new people, learn new skills, or give back to the community (or any combination of these)?

- Do you want to learn something new, or are you happy with your current skills and job?
- What's your passion, your unrealized dream? Do you want to be creative?
- Make a list of everything you love to do—both professionally and in your spare time. You might find something that will combine your present skills and a hobby you enjoy.

Continuing to Work in Your Long-Term Career

I love my work! And I continue studying so I can give my best. Of course, I can't do what I did when I was twenty, but I still have a lot of energy because I take care of my health. I believe that's my obligation as a performer. And I love the pleasure it brings other people. I have every intention of continuing until God says it's time to stop or until I feel I'm no longer able to give it my best. I so admire Nancy Wilson, who was a friend of mine. She decided it was time to retire because her voice wasn't what it used to be, and she was having some health issues. That was a very brave and professional thing to do. I see other performers continue beyond the time they should retire, and it makes my heart sad for them when I see them on stage because they can't move well and their voices don't sound good. Some can't even sing the right notes. I think this does a disservice to their fans, so everyone suffers. Ironically, it isn't merely about age. Tony Bennett is a fantastic example. I saw him perform at ninety years old, and he was sensational. He takes care of his voice and is the ultimate professional. Another example of an ageless performer is Rita Moreno, who is also fabulous. So you see, it really isn't about age. It's about how you take care of yourself and how you respect your career and your fans.

If you love your job and are able to continue past retirement age, then you're fortunate and should work for as long as you want or can. Doing something you love is good for your health and your wallet! I know that for a fact! A University of Maryland study found that men and women who kept working after retirement had fewer diseases and disabilities than those who stopped working completely.

Having a fulfilling job you love and having more leisure time, however, are not necessarily mutually exclusive. If you decide you want to slow down a little but not stop altogether, consider the possibility of part time, job sharing, or if possible, working from home some days. Many employers now accommodate flexible arrangements so they can retain older workers, take advantage of their skills and experience while reducing their work hours or commuting time.

Try Something New

You may decide you've reached a point where you can't progress any further in your current career, or perhaps you'd like to try something completely new and different. Don't be intimidated by ageism in the workforce. If you're applying for jobs in new areas, use your age to your advantage. Reinforce the skill sets you've learned as well as your reliability, work ethic, and commitment to a job well done. It's important to keep up with the changes in your particular field.

If you're not sure what you would actually like to do, list all your skills, then list the kind of work that appeals. Put the two together and see what fits best. Remember when you're itemizing your skills, include your hobbies and leisure activities. They could be relevant to your new career. For example, if you've always worked in an office environment but your hobby is some kind of handicraft, you might find your new career working in a craft store, where you could combine your organizational skills with your experience of artisanship. It's also important to look at what you *didn't* like about your old job. If certain aspects stressed you out, avoid them when looking for new employment. Focus on what you love to do and what interests you. Enjoy this new phase of your life.

If you don't want to commit to working on regular days every week, think about holiday work or short-term contracting. Try to find something that fits in with your lifestyle.

Below are some ideas for jobs that might utilize your maturity and previous work experience, combined flexibility, and personal interests:

1. Become a freelance consultant. There are lots of jobs available in retail, office, or home. It might even be possible to become a freelance consultant with your previous employer. They might welcome your knowledge of the business and value your input based on your years of experience.

2. If you love the theater or music and live near any performing arts centers, concert venues, convention centers, or theaters, you should check the availability of work there. In the summer months, there's often seasonal work available at outside concert venues.

3. House sitting is a great way of experiencing a new town without having to pay for accommodations. You just have to be responsible enough to take care of someone's home while they're away.

4. Pet sitting is an animal lover's dream. You can either move into a customer's home or have the pet to stay with you. Dog walking is another great way to earn money (and get fit!). Another alternative for animal lovers is to see if there are any jobs available in your local animal shelter.

5. Seasonal or part-time work in the retail field is worth considering if you like people. Try to find something in a store that sells the kinds of items you would purchase. It will make the job more fun, and you'll be a better sales assistant.

6. If you live near a resort area, there could be plenty of opportunities for part-time or seasonal work there.

7. Work for a nonprofit organization that is involved in a cause close to your heart.

Volunteering

If you don't need an additional source of income, volunteering is a very satisfying way of spending your free time. A 2012 study at Rush University Medical Center found that having purpose in life delayed cognitive decline and promoted a more generally healthy life. Doing good for others is doing good for you!

Volunteer organizations, far from being ageist, actually welcome older workers. They recognize the wealth of experience and skills they bring to any group. Remember as a volunteer you can find a role that utilizes everything you learned in your previous career. Volunteer organizations are always looking for a broad spectrum of skills that range from actual care giving in the community to helping with finance, developing new programs and protocols, and fundraising. In many cases, the organizers themselves don't have enough time to attend to everything so they're very happy to offload some of the work to a volunteer who has the necessary experience.

If you're interested in becoming a volunteer, go to your local library or place of worship, or check online. You'll find a vast array of groups close to your home. Go to one or two meetings before you commit to anything. You have to feel comfortable with the work of the group, as well as liking your potential coworkers. And don't worry if you go to one or two and the fit isn't right for you. Just keep trying until you find something suitable.

If the arts interest you, many museums have recruitment programs for docents. It's a great way to learn about a subject you enjoy then communicate your knowledge and passion to others.

Mentoring is another great way to give back. Nowadays, one in three young people grow up without any kind of life coach—whether it's an involved parent, grandparent, or family friend. All of those young people are denied the wisdom of an older person who only has their interests at heart. Imagine how tough it must be to buy your first car, need help with career choices, or even find out how to budget or cook—how to learn some of the basic life skills that our parents or grandparents taught us. Mentors can step into that gap by being willing to share skills, knowledge, and expertise. Mentoring relationships are a shared opportunity for learning and growth. It's a real win-win situation with many mentors saying that the rewards they gain are as substantial as those for their mentees. There are many mentoring programs available, like Big Brothers Big Sisters of America and America's Promise: The Alliance for Youth. You can check online or ask at your local church or place of worship. They should be able to point you in the right direction.

Return to School

I've dealt with learning new things in another chapter, but I've put this in as a reminder that you have this option. That old adage "You can't teach an old dog new tricks" just isn't true! Learning is important at any age. Going back to school doesn't just stimulate the brain and give you purpose. It allows you to mix with different generations. That, in itself, is a learning process.

If you have a local college that is easy to get to from your home, check out the courses and see what you'd like to do. It might be something that could enhance your existing skills, or it might be something you've always wanted to learn but never had the time. Who knows? It could even lead to a new business or income stream. Alternatively, you could take an online course. Just make sure the online college is a reputable one that offers proper accredited courses.

Whatever you choose to do with yourself in your second act, the most important thing to remember is that you have to believe in yourself. You have so much to offer. Just take your time and find something rewarding and fulfilling.

Chapter 20

FRIENDS

riends are very precious. I have very few close friends, and most of them have been friends for life—well, forty years or more, which is a significant period of time. Most of them are on the east coast so I don't get to see them on a regular basis, but we talk on the phone often.

I define a friend as someone I can confide in and discuss anything with, someone I trust and who, in turn, can trust me. The older I get, the more important I realize loyalty is necessary in a relationship. I know things about people they wouldn't want anyone else to know! I have a couple of confidantes I can call at three or four in the morning—and that's very special. It would be hard for me to imagine what I'd do without those dear people who are always there for me. It's impossible to overestimate the importance in our lives of our old friends. Not only have we shared so many experiences, but also we have common values and interests that strengthen the bonds that have forged throughout the decades. I also have friends from very different walks of life—very few in show business.

When people talk about friends on social media, like Facebook, to me they are connections, maybe acquaintances, but certainly not friends in the true sense. I think they should have another name for friends on Facebook. Maybe they should be called "associates," so as not to confuse the real meaning of friendship. I had hundreds of friend requests on Facebook but very few actual friends on my site. Finally, I accepted the requests, but I don't check my site very often because I don't have the time. I certainly don't share personal things on such a public forum. If I have something personal to say, I will call a friend or speak in person. Friends are people you spend time with, people you talk to—not people who hit "like" on a social media site!

Spending time with buddies gives you an important reset. We all have those special friends with whom we can discuss anything. And as we all know, laughter is the best medicine—and we all laugh with our friends.

But things change for a lot of people. Sadly, there is an epidemic of loneliness in the USA. Over the years, children and friends move away, and a further toll is taken as a result of divorce and death. Retirees often lose touch with colleagues from work. Neighborhoods alter. In many areas, the old concept of neighborhoods doesn't even exist anymore. In large cities like Los Angeles, many people don't even know the names of their neighbors in apartments right next to them.

At the same time, the older we get, the more important friends become. So many older people make the mistake of moving to be closer to their children and grandchildren. But the truth is that by leaving your social group, you're really isolating yourself. We all love our families and want to spend time with them, but different generations have different needs. Your children are probably working hard, building their careers, and earning enough to support their families. Your grandchildren, no matter how much they love you, still have their own lives. Once the novelty of having you around has worn off, you might find yourself feeling very lonely. It makes much more sense to stay put and continue to enjoy your life and your independence. According to an April 2017 study sponsored by the National Institute on Aging, friendship is more important than family ties for older people.

Your friends are also more likely to influence you to make better choices. Isn't it fun to go for a walk or to the gym with a buddy? If you want to eat healthier, having a pal who'll join you and encourage you makes it so much easier. You're more likely to get out of the house if you're feeling a little down when you have to meet a friend. Ultimately, devoting time to a friendship is probably the best long-term investment you can make. There's no doubt that the happier you are, the healthier you are. And good friends are a rich source of happiness. More than that, according to AARP, women with large social networks reduce their risk of dementia by 26 percent. Additionally, other research shows that friendships can boost our health in other ways. Socializing can strengthen the immune system, help us recover more quickly from illness, lower blood pressure and the risk of heart disease, sharpen memory, and even help us get a better night's sleep. According to one study, people with strong connections to family and friends have a 50 percent greater chance of outliving those with fewer social ties.

Bearing all that in mind, we should look at two areas with regard to friendship in our second act. The first is how to ensure our current friendships continue to be strong and flourish. The second is to see how we can make new friends if we're seeking to extend our circle.

Cherishing Old Friends

Friendships take time and effort and should never be taken for granted. This includes reviving some old friendships that might have been very special but have somehow fallen by the wayside. Sometimes we get hijacked by life and, when we finally have time to take a breath, we realize we've lost some dear people who were very special to us. Keeping friendships, like everything else in life that's worthwhile, needs time, effort, and thought. Here are some suggestions to help you nurture your friendships and to let your friends know how much they mean to you:

- Stay in regular touch with your friends and plan to get together as often as you can. Be proactive.
- Phone. Don't text! We all like to hear the voice of a friend. This is such a change from those endless robocalls!
- Establish standing dates, like once-a-month movie nights or potluck dinner. And it doesn't even have to be that much of a commitment. Meeting for coffee is fine.
- Plan fun get-togethers based on mutual interests, like watching the Academy Awards, a big TV sporting event, or even the season finale of a popular series like *Downton Abbey* or *Game of Thrones*.
- Send handwritten notes. A text or social media posting is fine sometimes, but nothing says, "I truly care" or "Thank you" as well as a good, old-fashioned, handwritten note or card. I don't mean you have to send a note for everything but a thank-you for a special gift, a note saying "I'm thinking of you" when a friend is

going through a difficult time, a get-well card, or sometimes just a note saying how much you treasure the friendship.

- When you're buying a gift, make it something thoughtful. It doesn't have to be expensive. A box of your friend's favorite cookies; movie tickets; and a gift card for use in their favorite hobby, book, or specialty food store are all items that would be greatly appreciated. Or if you're a good cook, make something special.
- Communicate honestly. Sometimes, our friends hurt us or let us down. If you can't let it go and you're finding yourself getting angry and resentful but you really treasure your friend, talk it through. Choose the right time to explain your feelings in the context of the importance of the friendship.

New Friends

Nowadays, making friends isn't so easy. It used to be that we'd meet likeminded folk while we were waiting for the kids to come out of school or we connected with people in our workplace. Now more and more people work from home or are empty nesters, retirees, or caregivers helping out elderly relatives—all situations that complicate the process of making new friends. So what's the best way to reboot your social life? Here are few suggestions:

1. Join a local community organization.
2. Go to local classes where you're likely to meet a kindred spirit: art classes, dancing, yoga, or learning a new language.
3. Join a gym. Some health care plans include a no-cost membership to a participating gym or fitness location. Check your plan to see if you're eligible. Some gyms offer a senior discount!
4. Check out your local library and see if they have a book club you can join.
5. Take a look at meetups online. There will be countless lists of groups where you can meet people with similar interests, like walking or learning local history.
6. Volunteer. What can be better than doing something good for others and, at the same time, meeting new people?

7. Get involved with your faith community. Check out events happening at your local place of worship.

Unhealthy Friendships

Let's admit it. We all have had them. Those friends who we've known for years, have been through so much together, but now we just don't enjoy being with them. We stuck with the relationship out of loyalty, habit, or guilt. Maybe their lives haven't turned out as well as they'd hoped and they can't get over their anger and resentment—and we understand that. But do we need to spend our precious time with someone who makes us unhappy? Our emotional health is very important. We want our friends to celebrate our wins, share our joy, and understand why we're down. And we try to fulfill the same role for them. Sometimes we just have to rethink friendships. First of all, let's take a look at what constitutes an unhealthy friendship. Ask yourself the following questions:

- Do you always feel emotionally drained after spending time with them?
- Does everything have to be done their way? Do you always have to go to the restaurant/movie/event of their choice? Do they refuse to compromise in order to occasionally accommodate your wishes?
- Do they react with jealousy when you talk about your happiness or achievements?
- If you can't always do what they want when they want it, do they make you feel guilty?
- Is everything that goes wrong in their lives someone else's fault? Are they always the victim and never take responsibility for their own poor decisions?
- Are they always quick to criticize you but never compliment you?
- Do they only talk about themselves and complain about their lives and never ask what's happening in your life?

If the answer to some (or all) of these questions is yes, it's time to reassess this friendship. But that doesn't mean severing the ties. First, see if you can save the relationship. Try explaining your feelings in a loving, caring way. Who knows? They may have been totally unaware of their behavior.

Sometimes, that just doesn't work. You still dread it when they call and want to get together. So it might be time to admit to yourself this friendship just isn't working but you still don't want to hurt your old friend. Try disengaging gradually. Be gentle and nonconfrontational. To achieve this, begin by not being proactive. Don't call them to talk or make plans. When they get in touch with you, leave a few days before you respond. Make it a little more difficult to get together—you're busy for the next couple of weeks perhaps. If after a while if this they don't take the hint, you just might have to be very brave and sit down with them to explain your feelings. To prepare for that difficult meeting, write down some notes for yourself. Don't be emotional or accusatory. Say things like "You deeply hurt me when ..." or "I'm sure it was unintentional but ..."

If this friendship truly isn't salvageable, don't feel guilty. Life moves on. Relationships built around a common interest like work or children can be allowed to naturally fade. It doesn't devalue what you had. You can still treasure those fond memories.

And Finally

Women are complex, and we all have different life experiences, so we can always learn a great deal from our friends. But don't expect too much from them either. It's almost impossible to find someone who agrees with us about everything! Allow your buddies to disagree with you about your favorite movie or book or even with the way you're handling a difficult situation. Sometimes, hearing another perspective can be very helpful. Embrace those differences.

Inevitably, there are times when we disagree with our friends too. And sometimes we hurt each other without meaning to. How often have you been upset because a friend didn't call you when you were sick or when you had an important doctor's appointment? However hurtful that may be, can you honestly say you've never forgotten to do the same thing? No one person can fulfill all the needs of friendship. For instance, some friends are great listeners, some always make us laugh, and others are problem solvers who can see a clear path when everything seems so confusing. It's unlikely that you have one friend who is all three of those things—and who never forgets a birthday and is always punctual!

And finally, you can treat strangers like friends too. I don't mean you should be a sycophant, but if someone has clearly gone to a lot of trouble to look good, say so. Very few people bother nowadays, but just remember how great it feels when someone tells you how good you look. We never know about people we meet in passing. Perhaps they live alone and see few people. They may not have a loved one who'll tell them how pretty their outfit is or how nice their hair looks. Be that person. It won't just make them feel good, but you'll feel great too. Just be sincere and honest.

Chapter 21
LEARN SOMETHING NEW EVERY DAY

There's a huge difference between *getting* old and *growing* old. Getting old is, well, getting old! Growing old means you continue growing, keeping your mind active, helping others, enjoying life, and taking care of yourself. I always think of plants in this context: some get old and die while others that are trimmed and nurtured live longer. My mother had a vine in her hospital room when she died. I brought it home and have cherished it for over eight years. It's flourishing and keeps getting new green shoots. Well, we humans are like that plant. I like to think I'm still growing and getting new leaves!

Of course, unlike the plant, just being taken care of physically doesn't prevent aging. Our minds need to be nourished too. I talk in a later chapter specifically about brain exercises, but here I want to explain the value of learning something new every day—using muscle memory to reconnect with the passions of our earlier years. I've always loved language and reading, so I like to learn new words every day. I like doing quizzes involving vocabulary. Sometimes, in my Bible readings I'll come across a word I don't really understand and check it out in the dictionary. I keep a dictionary and a Bible in each room and a thesaurus on my desk (and reading glasses too!). *Reader's Digest* has a section called "Word Power" every month. It makes it fun to learn new words.

Remember when we were kids? Every day was filled with new experiences. And I'm not talking just about school. Even summer vacation days were bursting with exciting new knowledge, whether it was learning to swim, walking in the woods and finding an interesting flower or bug, learning a new game, or strolling along a city sidewalk and having a friend point out something we'd never noticed before. All day, every day, our young minds were absorbing and processing new information, yet we had no idea this was happening. Then we became adults and all that changed. Our time became taken up with making a living, supporting ourselves and our families, and having demanding routines that eliminated me time. We just didn't have the time to be curious anymore. The sad thing about this is that studies have shown that learning new skills and embracing new ideas are important for our happiness. Believe it or not, learning makes us happier. Apart from the obvious satisfaction of developing a new skill, there are so many upsides to learning something new.

- It gives you a fresh topic to discuss with friends and family—particularly if you have a significant other.
- You'll meet other likeminded people and make new friends.
- Your confidence will grow. As you master your new skills, you'll feel so good about yourself.
- You'll be setting a great example to your children and grandchildren. If you can learn, so can they!
- You might end up falling into a new source of income. You never know!
- The more you learn, the more you'll learn. By expanding your mind and absorbing new skills and concepts, you're also strengthening your neural pathways.

First Steps

In order to begin learning something new each day, you don't have to rush out and sign up for a course. Start slowly and open your mind.

- Take a fresh look at your surroundings. For example, if you go for a walk, look around you. Do you know the names of the plants and flowers along the way? If not, you can research them and learn about them. Perhaps there's some interesting architecture you've never really noticed before. You could research its history at the local library.
- Make a point of reaching out to new people in your workplace, your gym, or even your neighborhood. Interacting with people is

opening your mind to new ideas. Ask people about themselves, their hobbies, and their lives. If someone is from a different country or culture, ask about their experiences growing up. You'll be surprised at what you will learn.

- If you particularly enjoy a movie or TV series that takes place in a different time and place from where you live, research that period or the life of the main character. Read books to expand your awareness. It's a really painless and fascinating way to delve into history, because you already have a context and a visual image of the period.
- Apply any new knowledge you discover. When you're next with friends, introduce the subject into the conversation. It might open up a lively discussion.
- Read the papers and stay abreast of current events. But don't stick with the same source all the time. Try reading some online sites for different perspectives. And if a news item particularly interests you, find out some more about the subject. For example, if something interesting happened in Barcelona, do some research into the city and learn more about its history and culture. If food is your passion, study the popular regional dishes.
- If you like fiction and you read a book you particularly enjoy, try to delve a little deeper into the story. For instance, if the character travels to a city or works in a job that is interesting, follow up by reading a nonfiction book that gives you some background information.
- Listen to audiobooks while you're driving or commuting. If there's a book you've always wanted to read but found daunting, like *Moby Dick,* an audiobook is a wonderful way of attacking it!
- If gardening and horticulture interest you, check out local gardening clubs and community gardens. You'll learn all about what grows best locally, from people in the know.
- The internet can be your friend. There are lots of online learning resources available. Just browse with an open mind.
- If DIY is your thing, watch online instructional videos to learn some basic skills. From woodworking to cooking, creating

spectacular table settings, and fixing your washing machine, it's all out there.

- Improve your cooking skills. Try a different recipe every day or two. The great benefit is that you're not only doing something you enjoy, but you can feed your loved ones and friends at the same time. A definite win-win for everyone!
- If you already play a musical instrument but haven't kept up your practice, try rehearsing every day for fifteen minutes or so to refresh your skills.

Go Back to School

It's never too late to learn something new. Lots of campuses offer free or discounted tuition for seniors. There are now almost unlimited opportunities for older adults to explore any number of subjects in a more formal educational environment.

The big bonus gift if you attend classes to develop a specific skill set is that you'll probably have plenty in common with your fellow students and you could find new friends among them.

Before you sign up for your first class, here are some points for you to consider:

- Choose a subject that's always interested you or something you wished you had studied but couldn't. What is it that consistently jumps out at you when you're looking for a book to read or a movie to see or even if you're reading a newspaper or magazine? If you always gravitate toward one particular subject, that may well be the course for you.
- Maybe your interest isn't in the more conventional courses like archaeology, foreign languages, or music. If that's the case, something like public speaking, creative writing, or interior design might be worth considering.
- Start simple and work your way up! Don't sign up for five classes all requiring a huge intellectual effort or a lot of time. You'll most likely be discouraged and give up on them all. Try one class that

sounds really interesting, then sign up for a second if you're feeling confident.

- Persist. The first class you choose might not be right for you. You might not like the teacher, or the subject may be less interesting than you hoped. Try another class. You'll find a fit sooner or later.

However, if you're not ready or confident enough to commit to formal classes, consider looking for lectures online or going to your local library and seeing what educational DVDs they have. Attend occasional lectures at museums, community centers, libraries, and schools. Many of them offer opportunities to listen to interesting guest speakers. The same places also sometimes offer a good range of nonacademic classes like sculpting, pottery, and dance.

When you're learning something new, don't be afraid to make a fool of yourself! Embrace risk to create meaningful experiences and moments of joy. Let's face it. By now we've all done some pretty stupid things at times. So what do you have to lose if something doesn't work out as well as it might? Be ready to try something new. Steel yourself to say yes instead of no. Just because you've never done something doesn't mean you won't enjoy it. And who knows? You might even discover a talent you didn't know you possessed.

Explore your hidden talents. Do something you've always wanted to do but were too self-conscious to try: dance, stand-up comedy, join a choir, etc. Don't fear failure. What does it matter? What's the worst thing that can happen?

Sadly, we live in a world where people are labeled "creative" and "not creative." And we fall for that myth. The famous writer Kurt Vonnegut said,

> Practicing an art, no matter how well or badly, is a way to make your soul grow, for heaven's sake. Sing in the shower. Dance to the radio. Tell stories. Write a poem to a friend, even a lousy poem. Do it as well as you possibly can. You will get an enormous reward. You will have created something.

So many people say, "I can't dance," "I can't sing," "I can't write," or "I can't perform," but many of us have never taken the opportunity to spread our wings. We just say we can't do something whereas we've never tried. Eventually it becomes a self-fulfilling prophecy. So when it comes to creativity, don't use "I can't" to mask your fear. Expressing yourself creatively doesn't have to be financially successful. It can be something you do for the sheer joy of accomplishment. If you attend an art class, for example, you don't have to consider whether your work will be critically acclaimed. Just enjoy the creative process. The same applies to learning a musical instrument or writing a book.

Once you stop fearing failure and embrace the satisfaction of developing a dormant talent, you will be truly liberated, and you will flourish.

Social Media

"The Americans have need of the telephone, but we do not. We have plenty of messenger boys." Thus said Sir William Preece in 1878 England. In the 1880s, Thomas Edison said, "The phonograph has no commercial value at all." He also declared, "The radio will die out in time!" Oh, if these gentlemen could experience the technology of today! What would they think of television, the computer, and the internet?

Webster's dictionary defines *social media* as interaction among people in which they create, share, and/or exchange information. This interaction happens in many ways: through online social networks, such as Twitter, Facebook, TikTok, Instagram, LinkedIn, YouTube, Pinterest, Snapshot, Skype, and many others. And the list of networks and ways of sharing grows almost daily. These networks can be effective communication for families, businesses, nonprofit organizations, political organizations, and more. They can be used on computers and mobile devices, such as smartphones, iPads, tablets, and laptops. Methods of sharing are through written text, photos, videos, and even vocal commands. Social media has greatly changed how we interact with the world around us.

I used to be one of those seniors who resisted change, but now I enjoy learning the new technology (albeit slowly!). I've learned to be patient when the computer shuts down by itself and to enjoy the many things I can accomplish faster by using it! When the COVID-19 pandemic occurred,

I really enjoyed using Zoom to "visit" with my family and friends and to conduct business meetings. I must admit that I am still forming the habit of checking my emails daily and, as a result, have *thousands!*

Now I can hear the groans from a few of you seniors who are still as technically challenged as I was! Listen. If I can learn to use social media, *anyone* can! I suggest you do what I did. Actually, I did a combination of two things. I went to sites on the computer that explained how to use Zoom and I called upon young friends to help me with Facebook and email. Your grandchildren or other young people will enjoy teaching you something new, and it allows time for you to bridge the generational gap and bond with them. Most colleges have classes for seniors as do many organizations, such as AARP. DOROT is one organization that provides computer courses designed for seniors. This can be done from home with a computer and telephone. There are also instruction books, but I prefer one-on-one lessons.

Today, social networking has almost replaced the telephone, and it is really necessary for everyone to learn some form of social networking, as the advantages greatly outweigh the negative. Social networking can be a mental stimulant for seniors by introducing them to games they can play or to work opportunities. They can also stay informed about the latest news both with their families and friends and the world around them. They can even find long-lost family members or friends and make new friends. This is especially helpful for anyone who has mobility challenges and cannot get out of the house. I think one of the most advantageous things about the internet is the educational advantages that are available for both young and older people. Some of the key health benefits are reduction of loneliness, depression, and loneliness. And of course, the internet can be entertaining, with movies and videos available to watch and games to play.

While it is necessary to know about these sites and be familiar with their use, they should be used responsibly. Research has proved that although these sites can provide pleasure from sharing photos of family and friends and make doing business easier and more efficient, if misused, social media can become addictive and can cause loneliness and even emotional illness, such as anxiety and depression. After all, we humans were created to communicate with each other physically, not mainly with machines! There is also the possibility of harassment and fraud from information "hackers." When using the internet, you can choose how you want your personal information shared—with the general public or only those people you designate. We should enjoy social media without allowing it to become antisocial media!

Chapter 22

DECLUTTERING YOUR LIFE

Most of us collect stuff throughout our lives, then we sometimes have to reassess. When I moved to my new, smaller home, I had to give away many possessions. Fortunately, my condo provided room enough for all the items I really wanted, but it did force me to consider what I simply had to keep and what I could let go of. As I went through a lifetime of accumulated treasures, I realized I don't have difficulty parting with things when I know they're going to bring happiness to someone else.

When I was going through all the boxes of possessions I had accumulated, I decided if something brings me great joy, I'll keep it. There's still a lot of little girl in me, and I admit I just love toys. I had quite a large collection of clowns, many of which I gave away. I decided to keep the ones that were gifts from special people because they had great sentimental value. I've always liked clowns because no matter how a clown feels, they make people happy. They are true entertainers. I also inherited a doll collection that belonged to my mother. When she was a child, her sister used to rip up all my mother's dolls, so dolls were very special to her. I liked them too when I was a child, so when I grew up, I used to send dolls to my mother as gifts whenever I saw one I thought she'd particularly like. When I moved, I gave most of them away, but like the clowns, I kept a few special ones for myself. One of my favorite dolls is one I bought in a convent in LA. It's a very sweet doll that sings "You Raise Me Up."

How much stuff have you accumulated over the years? I bet it's quite a bit. As we get older, things seem to arrive on our doorsteps. Beloved parents, relatives, and friends pass on and leave us their treasures. And we do treasure them—but perhaps for the wrong reasons. Do you really need that vase or dinner service? Clutter can be confusing, and too much clutter can be utterly paralyzing. If you have stuff in boxes that you haven't opened in years, the chances are it's time to get rid of the contents. Old magazines and birthday cards (unless they're particularly sentimental) should be consigned to the recycling bin.

Getting rid of sentimental items can be very difficult, but one way of doing it is by expressing gratitude for the joy that item once gave you. For example, if it's your mother's dinner service that you never use but can't bear to give away, spend some time thinking about the wonderful family meals you had and the happy times you all shared together. Say thank-you, first offer it to family members, then if no one wants it, give it to Goodwill or some other charity, content in the knowledge that another family will create their own happy memories from your gift. And don't cheat. Just putting stuff in bags and boxes then putting it back in the closet doesn't count!

A fun way of getting rid of treasured but no longer wanted items is to throw a declutter party. If you're moving and you want to get rid of lots of things, invite your friends over and let them choose some items that remind them of happy times they've spent in your home with you. You'd be surprised how much enjoyment you'll get and how much funky stuff you dispose of.

Declutter Your Home

If your home is in chaos, there's a good chance your mind is too! Clear your environment, and it will help you to focus on more important things than hunting for that important document or trying to remember where you last saw your keys.

Once you make the decision to declutter or, as I prefer to say, simplify, your home, take it one small step at a time. If you set out to tackle every room and closet over one weekend, the task will be too big and intimidating. The chances are you'll give up quite quickly.

Here are a few simple tips to conquer the clutter and embrace simplicity in your home:

- As I've said above, take it one room at a time (or part of a room like a desk, work area, or closet). Or if you prefer, set for yourself a time limit. Decide you're going to spend an hour sorting out two drawers, for example. Your goals should be achievable.
- Make sure you clear plenty of space in which to work. You'll need room to make three piles: keep, throw away, and donate.
- Empty out your drawers, and sort them the same way as above. Just removing things from a surface and shoving them out of sight in a drawer doesn't count as decluttering!
- With each item, ask yourself if you really need it, if you use it regularly, and/or if you love it. If your answer is no, get rid of it.
- Make sure you dispose of your throwaway and donation piles at the end of each session. Otherwise, you're just moving the clutter and keeping things you don't love or need.
- Get help from a trusted friend who will be honest about whether you should keep or throw away some of your possessions. My sister Bernadette was a big help to me.
- Once your home is organized, remember the mantra "Don't put it down. Put it away." It will help you to keep everything in its designated space.
- Are you always losing your keys? Putting them down somewhere then forgetting where they are? Put a pretty box or small basket on the hall table or some surface near the front door and train yourself to drop your keys in there as you walk into your home. Eventually, it will become automatic and will prevent that last-minute panic as you dash out the door and realize your keys are nowhere to be found.
- Do you have to play "hunt my glasses" several times a day? The same principle applies. Find an attractive box or basket and leave it beside your workspace or TV chair so you'll always be able to find them. I have inexpensive pairs of reading glasses in every room.

Your Work Desk or Work Area

When I moved, I had years and years' worth of papers, and they were the most difficult things to get rid of. I had to go through all of them because they had personal information, so it all had to be properly shredded. But your desk or work area isn't just about papers. If you want to be the most productive and focused you can, having a clear, organized work area is essential. Here are a few tips to help you get your work area in order:

- Make sure you have attractive, matching containers for pens, paper clips, etc. They'll look good and immediately start creating some order on your desk.
- Have good old-fashioned in and out boxes. They can be simple and functional from an office supply store, or you can use pretty baskets or boxes if you prefer.
- Get drawer dividers so you won't have to go hunting through a messy drawer for that one item you're seeking.
- Set up an alphabetical filing system, and label files clearly.
- When papers come in, file them immediately. Don't just pile everything up again. You'll save so much time later.

Declutter Your Mind

Now that you've started thinking about decluttering your surroundings, it's time to move on to the real purpose of this chapter, which is to clear your mind. Removing clutter from your life or embracing simplicity doesn't just refer to your home or office. It also applies to your brain and the way you live your life. We all have so much "garbage" spinning round in our brains, jumbling up our thoughts that sometimes simple decision-making seems almost impossible.

Let's begin with managing your time.

- Acknowledge the value of your time. Time is very precious, and as we get older, we just can't afford to waste hours or days doing things that are unproductive or don't give us joy, happiness, or satisfaction.
- Look at your calendar and make a list of all your activities. Then divide them into the things you have to do (work, medical appointments, etc.), things you want to do (meeting friends, hobbies, classes, etc.), and the things you don't have to do. Identify what you want to do, and eliminate the rest.

- Reduce your commitments. Learn to say no to things you really don't want to do. You'll have so much more time to do what you love or spend time with the people who bring you joy.
- Analyze your routines. Try to bring structure into them by designating one day for housework, shopping, or whatever tasks you have to complete on a regular basis.
- Make lists. Whether they're to-do lists or shopping lists, it's so much easier to be organized when everything you need to achieve is written down. As you complete each task, just cross it off. You'll have great satisfaction (and a better night's sleep) knowing that you won't suddenly remember something important that you failed to do.

Here are a few tips to help manage your mind and help you plan for a simpler, happier, more productive lifestyle:

- Set priorities. Make a list of all the tasks you have to achieve—long and short term—and prioritize them. Set goals for yourself, whether it's weight loss, fitness, reading a book, learning to cook Italian, or traveling to another country.
- Look at your task list and analyze how you can achieve those goals. Is it as simple as shopping for ingredients, joining a gym, going to the library, or signing up for a course? If it's travel, do you need to get a passport? If it's work oriented, do you need to study a subject in order to increase your knowledge? Write down how you plan to accomplish your aim.
- Keep a journal. Writing out your thoughts is very good therapy. It's a way of dealing with negative influences and working through problems, therefore reducing stress. Just reading what you have written can sometimes clarify your thoughts and indicate a clear path through to problem solving.
- Try to think positively rather than negatively. If a colleague at work is annoying, try to look at his or her positive qualities rather than allowing irritating habits to get under your skin. If you're stuck in traffic, use the time to listen to your favorite music or audiobook. Negativity and anger are so exhausting!

- Make a daily to-do list, and do one thing at a time. As we get older, multitasking becomes less productive, but we all do it. If you're tackling one task, see it through to the end before you move on to the next. It's so much simpler.
- Stop and take some deep breaths. It helps you both physically and mentally to relax and let go of the stress.
- Make decisions. If you tend to be indecisive, take a pen and paper and draw a vertical line down the middle of the page. Write the pros on one side and the cons on the other. A complicated choice can be so much simpler when you can clearly see the options on both sides.
- Share your thoughts with friends and loved ones. You don't have to keep everything in your head.
- Take a break from TV and social media. Sometimes it's okay to let the world turn a couple of times without actively participating!
- Find some alone time. Take a walk, have a nap, take some time out to pray, or meditate. Your batteries need recharging just as much as any cell phone.
- If you love to read, do so selectively. Don't just devour every book that comes your way. It's better to read a good book slowly than a bad book quickly.
- Don't overcommit. If you feel stressed just looking at your calendar, eliminate some of your commitments. If that's difficult, at least make sure you allow plenty of time between each appointment. By eliminating the stress of worrying about sitting in traffic or finding a parking space, you'll arrive in a much better mindset with more energy to focus on the event you're attending, whether it's a meeting, a dinner with a friend, or a playdate with grandchildren.
- Spend time in nature when you can. Walking in a city park or woods or by the sea is naturally calming and helps eliminate all the stimuli that constantly bombard us in our day-to-day lives.

Chapter 23

SPIRITUALITY AND MINDFULNESS

Charm is deceitful and beauty is passing, but a woman
who fears the Lord, she shall be praised.

—Proverbs 31:30 (NKJV)

I have combined spirituality and mindfulness because I feel one can
influence the other. By practicing mindfulness, I believe you can
achieve an inner peace and calm that can lead to a higher level of
spirituality.

Spirituality

I vividly remember the morning when I looked at myself in the mirror and
realized that I was no longer a girl but a mature woman. In fact, I looked
just like my mother! It was scary! I told that woman in the mirror, "Girl,
it's time you put aside some of your concentration on makeup and hair
and focus more on your inner beauty."

Spiritual beauty is that beauty which radiates from a person from the
Holy Spirit who dwells within us. It is influenced by one's character (or
lack of) and is the most important type of beauty. Have you ever seen a
gorgeous woman who attracted the attention of everyone but as soon as
she opened her mouth and revealed her spirit, everyone was turned off?

You may have noticed that I have mentioned God frequently
throughout this book. That's because He is the very most important
thing in my life, and this strongly influences my ideas on beauty. Most of

us don't even think about what, besides physical appearance, attracts us to people (especially someone of the opposite sex). Stop and think. Don't you just feel comfortable being in the presence of certain people? That's because they have a good spirit. You hear people say that this book or that is their Bible. Well, the Bible is my Bible! Proverbs 10–31 (NKJV) tells us what constitutes a beautiful woman. My favorite verse is 30, which says, "Charm is deceitful and beauty is passing."

The cultural details of her specific tasks are different in our era, but the principles are timeless because they speak of a virtuous woman valued above rubies. The biblical David was an example of a spiritually beautiful man.

Some of the things that determine spiritual beauty are the following:

- your attitude: how you react to situations
- your heart: do you do deeds just to please others and receive compliments, or do you do things with an open heart?
- generosity of time, deeds, money, and possessions
- compassion
- kindness
- gentleness
- grace

I think this quotation from the Bible says it all:

"Do not let your adornment be merely outward – arranging the hair, wearing gold, or putting on the fine apparel—rather let it be the hidden person of the heart, with the incorruptible beauty of a gentle and quiet spirit, which is very precious in the sight of God." (1 Peter 3:3–4 NKJV)

In 1985, I cohosted a television show with Sammy Davis Jr. During his introduction of me, Sammy said I was the spiritual member of The 5th Dimension. How did he know? At the time, I was only one of two Christians in the group, and a "closet Christian" at that. I wrongly kept my spirituality to myself and did not share my faith with others. Perhaps a glimmer of God's light showed through my actions, but I don't really know what he knew or saw in me. I do believe that spiritual beauty is measured more by our actions than mere thoughts. Sometimes God will place us in situations in which we have a chance to let our spiritual beauty shine—a family or business crisis, for instance. How do you handle adversity? Are you calm? Do you listen before speaking? Do you *hate the sin but love the person?* Are you judgmental? It's so much easier to love others if you first love God and then accept and love yourself.

I highly suggest that you find a place of worship that nourishes you spiritually. Find a park or quiet place (maybe in your home) where you can meditate. Get a prayer partner for added strength. How you express your spirituality is a very personal thing, but as your spirituality grows, watch your beauty shine. As Victor Hugo wrote, "Good actions are the invisible hinges on the doors of heaven."

I usually spend the first hour of the day in prayer, Bible reading, and devotion, beginning at six o'clock in the morning—sometimes with one of my prayer partners. This fortifies me and gets my day started on a positive and inspirational note. I also have my own devotional reading and personal prayers later in the day. These habits have sustained me through many hard and trying times and made life much more beautiful for me. Attending church on Sunday mornings and Thursday afternoons is also something I look forward to. There was a time when, because of a bad experience, I stopped attending church. I also used the excuse that often The 5th Dimension performed on Saturday nights and I was too tired to get up to go to church on Sunday. One day, the Lord showed me how He had been there for me *every* day, no matter what. Couldn't I give Him just one or two hours a week? Since that time, I have made it a habit to attend church on Sunday, no matter where in the world I am. Now this doesn't make me any better than someone who does not attend church, but fellowshipping with other believers gives me strength and courage to face the rest of the week. Sometimes, because of my performance schedule, I have to "have church" with The 5th Dimension members or whomever I am with. "Church" doesn't have to always happen in a church building!

A few examples of spiritually beautiful people are Mother Teresa, Nelson Mandela, Jack Hayford, Stevie Wonder, and Billy Graham. Although they're from different worlds, all are examples of spiritually beautiful people.

There were some wonderful people who influenced me spiritually. I didn't realize it at the time, but my grandmother paved the way for the growth of my spiritual beauty. As a matter of fact, as a child, I though it funny when she, an old lady of sixty, graduated from Bible school. I thought only children and young people attended school. She prayed with and for me and instilled in me that "pretty is as pretty does."

My mother was not as openly spiritual, but I know now that she prayed for me all the time. The results are very apparent. When I went through her Bible after she died, I found wonderful letters she had written to God. She prayed for others and thanked God for sparing her life so she could raise her children. When she was in the last stages of cancer, the doctors gave her four months to live, but God allowed her to live forty years and enjoy not only her children but her grandchildren and great-grandchildren. She told Him she wanted to win the lotto so she could help people of all nationalities!

Jack Hayford, who was the senior pastor at the Church on the Way in Van Nuys, California, was one of my biggest nonfamily spiritual influences. I believe this is because I was ready to grow spiritually. I was sincerely seeking the Lord. Pastor Jack, as he was affectionately called, was a wonderful teacher. Highly intellectual, he knows the scriptures well and, as a matter of fact, edited my favorite study Bible. He was also a compassionate counselor and helped me during some very difficult times in my life. Pastor Jack, through his living example, also taught me, among other things, two very important life lessons: humility and how to truly serve others. I also have faithful "prayer partners" around the country who pray with and for me.

Some people set aside certain times of the day for prayer. This is a good practice and a way to get into the habit of "praying without ceasing." Try devoting set times of each day to thank God for your blessings. You can do this no matter what religion you are or what you are going through. If you're an atheist, use that time to meditate on the good things in your life. It has been medically proven that praying and meditating are good for the health. It calms the nerves and contributes to a healthy heart and mind.

Some people think that the word *meditate* only relates to new age religion, but the Bible states to meditate on God's principles (Psalm 119:23, 48), meditate through the night (Palm 63:6), and meditate on God's great works (Psalm 143:5 NKJV).

As I said previously, I usually begin my day with prayer and meditation at 6:00 a.m. I start this early so I am not rushed and while it is still quiet, with no phones or doorbells ringing. This really strengthens me for the rest of the day. I do feel a difference if I don't ask the Lord to bless my day. I don't have a set length of time for prayer. It varies from thirty minutes to over an hour. Sometimes I combine my prayer with exercise and take a prayer walk. I have to be flexible, especially when I'm traveling. I used to do this alone, but now I have prayer partners. There's strength in numbers, and when two or three are gathered together, the Spirit of the Lord is really strong.

I also often stop in the middle of the day to give thanks, and I end my day with prayer. Frequently, many times during the day, I find myself just thanking God for something: my sight, good health, my home, etc. In fact, I thank Him for any number of good things in my life. This may seem like just a habit to you, and it may be. But it's a *good* habit and, because it's from the heart, yields many positive results.

One of my favorite things to do in my spare time is to read inspirational books. I mentioned before that one of my favorite authors is Og Mandino. Others are Jack Hayford, Billy Graham, Stormie Omartin, Joyce Myers, and TD Jakes.

You should take time to check your spiritual heart as often as you check your physical self. This is the deepest part of you, your attitude, your motives for doing things. (Psalm 51:10 NKJV)

Mindfulness

As you can see, spirituality is an essential part of my life. One path to achieving spirituality is to pursue mindfulness, which helps you to concentrate on the present and gain a better perspective on life. It's important to enjoy every moment of your life and focus on the positive, even during tough times. Begin with this simple breathing technique: Spend five minutes a day focusing on your breathing. Close your eyes and take some deep breaths. Be aware of each breath coming in and going out. If thoughts crowd in, acknowledge them, then let them go and refocus on your breathing. Breathe in the positive and out the negative.

If you get stressed or overwhelmed during the day with lots of thoughts swirling around your brain, it's a simple matter to take a minute or so and practice this technique to calm yourself and refocus your mind.

Here are some tips to help you concentrate on what's important and eliminate some of the negative thoughts and fears we all have:

- Pay attention to your posture. If you're constantly walking around with hunched shoulders or clenched fists, take a deep breath and change your posture. Stand straight, unclench your fists, and smile. Your body can fool your mind into believing you're relaxed!
- Change self-critical thoughts into positive ones. If you're feeling gloomy or pessimistic, think of something positive. It can be as simple as appreciating getting to work on time because there was no traffic or picturing the greeting you'll get from your dog when you arrive home.
- Don't try to be too perfect. I know that society seems to demand perfection from all of us (think of those airbrushed photos of celebrities), but looking good is just fine. There are very few things in life that are perfect. It's okay to strive for perfection, but be happy doing your best.
- Gratitude journaling is a really helpful method of appreciating all the positive things in your life. Write down what you're grateful for.
- Each morning, say thanks for five things for which you're grateful. Don't make it overly complicated. It could be as simple as seeing the sunshine outside your window or enjoying your coffee before you head out for the day.
- Allow yourself to feel disappointed. Accept it, and move on. It's just another learning experience.
- Congratulate yourself. You're doing the best you can.
- Make your home a refuge from the world. Surround yourself with items that make you happy, but don't get too cluttered!
- Don't be too harsh on yourself. You're trying hard to be the best person you can be. And don't pretend to be something you're not. The original you is just fine!
- Don't let other people put you down. That means they have a problem, not you.
- If you're tense, try forest bathing. It's a delightful Japanese term for walking in the woods or in a green space. The University of Exeter Medical School has found that two hours a week spent in

nature are good for health and mental well-being. You don't have to spend the two hours all in one time. Fifteen minutes a few times a week is all you need.

- Be still for some part of every day.
- Focus on the now. Stop thinking about where else you could be or what else you should be doing.
- Treat yourself the way you treat a friend. Don't be cruel or hypercritical.

Chapter 24

THE FIVE SENSES

We have been blessed with five senses: sight, hearing, touch, smell, and taste. Think for a moment just how important each of those senses are to us and the joy they bring us. When we see our baby for the first time, hear a glorious piece of music, feel the touch of a loved one, smell a rose, or bite into a ripe peach and taste the sweet flavor, we can savor those moments because we have our five senses. I believe God speaks to us through our senses so in the following pages, I show some ways one can enhance one's spiritual beauty using the five senses we have been blessed with.

Sight

Never lose an opportunity of seeing everything that is beautiful; for beauty is God's handwriting—a wayside sacrament.

Welcome it in every fair face, in every fair sky, in every fair flower; and thank God for it as a cup of blessing. (Ralph Waldo Emerson)

Vision is incredibly complex, and sight is thought to be the most developed of the human senses. It is said that the eyes are the windows of the soul. In which case, it's important to keep your windows clean! Be selective when you're choosing television programs, movies, etc. Many of us innocently watch television programs that disrespect the family—that show children being insolent toward their parents, wives and husbands dishonoring their mates, and friends betraying friends for the sake of comedy. We may think these programs are funny, but this is a subliminal way of condoning disrespect of the family and, I believe, promotes the disruption and even breakup of the family unit. Be selective with what you read too. Books, magazines, commercials, and even billboards contain all kinds of inappropriate messages. Some people think that it's okay to read anything because reading is education, but I don't agree. Reading trash is putting trash into your brain. In this instance, "Garbage in, garbage out" is not necessarily true! Garbage in, garbage *stored* is more accurate!

Close the shutters on negative or vulgar sights. Lock out the vision of unnecessary violence. I believe that if we don't do this, our children are in danger of becoming desensitized. Violence has become acceptable in the media and has even been turned into extremely cruel video games. Think back to your childhood. Do you realize that TV heroes like the Lone Ranger did not kill anyone? Now our children play games where the object of winning is to kill as many people as possible. No wonder there is so much violence on the streets and in the home. And it is not necessary to sneak into porn shops or movies these days. Television and the internet have brought pornography right into our homes, available to adults and children to watch on the television and computer. So protect that precious gift of sight, and try to make sure you see beauty rather than ugliness, even when you're relaxing in front of the television or heading out to the movies.

Sound

"Sound" is a catch-all word which describes "all that we hear," in one lump, from music to noise. (Anita T. Sullivan)

Sound is another very important sense. As we all know, what we hear so easily sets the mood for us. Beautiful music is soothing and uplifting, while ugly, discordant sounds set our nerves on edge. But it isn't just the sound itself that affects us. We're living in times when it is difficult to go through a day without hearing anything negative or vulgar. Try it yourself. Walk around and try listening—really listening—to what you're hearing, what people are saying. Whether in the grocery store, driving, or just walking down the street, I assure you that you will hear someone using vulgar language or speaking negatively. Believe it or not, I've even heard negativity in the parking lot of the house of worship.

Since you can't control what you hear from others, you must filter out these words and replace them with positive thoughts and prayers for those who use them. Turn an ugly moment into something beautiful by making it an opportunity to minister. For example, I was in line at a public outdoor event with my son when he was around ten years old. The teenage boys behind us began talking loudly, using profanity. I turned to them and said, "Don't you boys see a lady and a child? Please watch your language." They immediately apologized. They were so used to using that kind of language, they weren't even aware that it was vulgar, which is desperately sad. My son said, "Mom, maybe their mothers allow them to talk like that." I simply replied, "Well, they're not home, and I'm not their mother!" Unfortunately, these days, we do have to be careful to whom we speak and what we say, but adults should take the responsibility for teaching young people. "Let the words of my mouth and the meditations of my heart be acceptable in Your sight, O Lord, my strength and redeemer" (Psalm 19:14 NKJV).

Music is a very important element of what we hear, because it can paint a picture of where we were when we heard a particular song and what we were feeling. I can see so clearly in my mind's eye exactly where I was when I first heard Stevie Wonder's "I Just Called to Say I Love You!" I remember being shocked when I anticipated the last three notes without ever having heard the song! It has been scientifically proven that different types of music provoke different feelings. For instance, classical music is soothing while rock music can provoke anger and/or confusion. The next time you visit a shopping mall or department store, notice what kind of music is playing. In fact, music is so important that it can encourage people to spend money. The happy Christmas music around the holidays makes people want to shop so business improves for the storeowners. And what would the movies be like without music? The movie *Jaws* wouldn't have been half as scary without the music.

One of the reasons The 5th Dimension has had a successful career for over fifty years is because our music makes people feel good. I remember being skeptical when a young lady told me she had every intention of committing suicide but then she heard The 5ᵗʰ Dimension singing "Up, Up, and Away" on the radio and decided not to take her life. I thought she was exaggerating, but several other people have told me a similar story. How proud I am to be a part of such positive influence.

> She had a acute ear, and tiny sounds, the shiver of grass in light airs, the squeaking of bats, cries of birds in a distant field, creaking of dried roots, the trickle of rain down the walls of a house, were caught by it, and offered to memory. (Storm Jameson)

Others have expressed the importance of silence much better than I have. Several references from my favorite book are "To everything there is a season. A time to keep silent, and a time to speak" (Ecclesiastics 3:7) and "In the multitude of words sin is not lacking, but he who restrains his lips is wise" (Proverbs 10:19). And my favorite saying is this: "It is better to remain silent and thought a fool than to speak up and remove all doubt" (Maurice Switzer). "He who has knowledge spares his words, and a man of understanding is of a calm spirit. Even a fool is counted wise when he holds his peace; when he shuts his lips, he is considered perceptive" (Proverbs 17:27–28 NKJV). How true that is.

So here's something I recommend you do. Try turning off the radio and television and any other device for just one day and enjoy the silence. I so like waking up in the morning and hearing the birds on my balcony. What a beautiful way to break the silence of the night.

Touch

> We are forever in the dark about what touch means to another. With touch, one enters at once a private and an ambiguous world. (Jessamyn West)

Touch is generally considered to be the first sense that humans develop. Babies feel their mother's touch and respond positively to being gently stroked and kissed. I do believe that how we are treated in childhood has a big influence on our desire to be touched as an adult. My mother was not a hugger, but my father was. As I grew up, I often gave the wrong signal to male friends by having what I meant as a friendly hug mistaken for a sexual advance!

And as we grow, we all continue to need some form of touch. I am a hugger and like to be touched by those I like but can't stand for strangers to touch and grab me. This is difficult for me in the business I am in. Often after a show, people will come up to me and grab my arm or pull me toward them for a hug. Now I know how babies may feel with people pinching their cheeks! In fact, a little, old lady actually did that to me once!

It is important for children to see affection between their parents. Just think how heartwarming it is when you see an elderly couple walking hand in hand. Young married couples need to take time for each other and practice this simple habit. It's hard to stay mad with someone when you're holding hands!

On the other hand, I think some young people do a bit too much touching! Some of them need to learn to respect each other and reserve intimate touching for marriage or at least to keep it private. I know it probably sounds old-fashioned, but I really don't think it's appropriate to make out in full view of the public.

When used at the proper time in the proper situations, touch can be beautiful. It can even be a mental thing. In this case, it could mean to affect or influence, as in that music "touched" me. Do your actions "touch" people in a beautiful way? How do your words "touch" others? I think the old saying "Sticks and stones can hurt my bones, but words will never hurt me" is completely untrue. Words can actually hurt much more than "sticks and stones" and for a much longer time. Physical bruises heal and are generally quickly forgotten, but it's very hard to forget the damage done by cruel words.

Taste

No argument can persuade me to like oysters if I do not like them. In other words, the disturbing thing about matters of taste is that they are not communicable. (Hannah Arendt)

A smart woman will learn her man's favorite tastes. There's a lot of truth to the old saying "The way to a man's heart is through the stomach!" Oh! The power of a good apple pie!

The tongue is the body's organ that is used to taste. It is sensitive to sweetness, saltiness, sourness, and bitterness. Our sense of taste and smell are closely related. Just think how you feel when you smell bread baking; you can almost taste the bread on your tongue. Or think how repelled you are by food that smells horrible. There's no way you can eat it.

But the tongue isn't just about taste. It's one of the most important organs of the body—and the hardest to "tame!" The Bible has much to say about the tongue, and if one is to be spiritually beautiful, one should take heed. "Life and death are in the power of the tongue." In other words, what one says to or about a person can either build and/or encourage him or her or discourage or bring him or her down. How often we will thoughtlessly say something and then say, "I was only joking" or "You know I didn't mean that!" But it's already been said and we cannot take back the words once spoken!

As I said previously, sticks and stones can break our bones, but words can also injure or even kill. People's spirits can be completely destroyed by cruel words. It is important to be aware of what we say and how we say it. After someone sees us, what we say is the next impression that person has of who we are. Are you giving a beautiful, positive first impression? Or do you find yourself always having to do damage control? Are you one of those people who say what you mean, or do you tell people what you think they wish to hear from you? Have you ever attended the funeral of a loved one and thought, *I wish I had told him (her) how much I loved him (her)*? Do the words you speak leave a good "taste"?

Other definitions for *taste* are "to partake of" or "a bit." But the definitions I want to expound on are sense of beauty, discernment, correctness, judgment, decorum, and manners. There are actions and sayings that are in good taste in some cultures but bad taste in others. For example, making a zero with the forefinger and thumb means okay in some cultures but something quite vulgar in others. And there are things that used to be considered good taste in our society that have been forgotten—or perhaps never taught—by many younger people of today.

For example, I rarely see a young man pulling out the chair for a lady before sitting down himself, and opening doors for ladies seems to be a thing of the past.

Smell

> Smell is a potent wizard that transports us across thousands of miles and all the years we have lived. (Helen Keller)

According to some research, we humans can smell over 1 trillion scents with our four hundred smelling receptors. No wonder cleanliness is so important. Almost every day, someone tells me I smell good. I believe that, as a lady, I am *supposed* to have an attractive fragrance. I don't mean with a heavy perfume that people can smell before I get within two feet of them but a "sweet smell" that is noticed if I am in close proximity or give someone a hug. I am actually more comfortable going out without makeup than I am leaving home without my fragrance! Unfortunately, because I have been wearing the same fragrance for years, I'm no longer aware of my perfume so I have to be careful not to put on too much, which as we all know can be quite offensive.

Since everyone's body chemistry is different, each person has to find a fragrance that is compatible with his or her body. (And yes, men should smell good too!) Scents bring back memories, like cookies baking or lovely, warm, Christmassy smells. I am really turned off by a man who wears a heavy aftershave. I much prefer a more natural, freshly showered fragrance. For me, the old-fashioned "Old Spice" cologne does just this. I'm sure that is because, as a little girl, I used to love sitting and watching my father shave, after which he would put on Old Spice After Shave!

One important point to remember when you're buying perfume is that perfumes smell different on different people. Just because someone you know always wears the most attractive perfume, it doesn't mean it will be good on you. We all have our own individual mix of hormones and pheromones that alter the way fragrances smell on different skin. The best thing to do is to test a perfume in a store. If it smells good there, don't rush and buy it. Let it stay on your skin for a couple of hours. Does it still smell good, or has it faded and changed? You should also ask a close friend or partner for their opinion. It can be very difficult to know exactly how a fragrance smells on your own body.

It is also important that your surroundings smell good. When I travel, I carry scented candles so that my hotel room will have a sweet fragrance. My favorites are the Gardenia soy candle from Archaeology and Midnight Jasmine by Yankee Candles.

Finally, the Bible speaks of the gospel as "the fragrance of Christ" (1 Corinthians 2:15 NKJV). That's one "fragrance" I enjoy every day, all day!

Chapter 25

THE BRAIN

⸻⸻⸻◇◇◇⸻⸻⸻

We have to take care of our brains just like every other part of our body. We have to nourish, exercise, and rest them. No matter how trim your body, youthful your face, or stylish your clothes may be, if your brain isn't alert and curious, you'll be less attractive.

Of course, my work keeps me active mentally as well as physically, but even in my leisure time, I try to challenge my brain. I like to do all kinds of games and crossword puzzles. *Wheel of Fortune* is one of my favorite shows because I play against the contestants. In my quiet moments, I read a great deal. If I want to be more social, I enjoy playing cards or Monopoly with friends, which is always a good way to keep my mind sharp.

But no matter how engaged we are, let's admit, we may have senior moments! All those times we walk into the kitchen or bedroom to get something then we can't remember what it is we were looking for. That's so frustrating, but it doesn't mean our brains are failing. Forgetting things is very common, especially nowadays when we're in a permanent state of sensory overload. And of course, aging does have an effect on the brain. The bad news is that our brains reach their maximum size in our early twenties, but the good news is that they're also capable of regrowth. That means we can continue to learn and acquire new skills throughout our lives. And we can help that process by taking care of our brains and ensuring we participate in brain-boosting activities, which should be challenging, involve learning something new, and be rewarding so you get satisfaction out of the experience. Whenever you push yourself, your brain is building new cell connections, which is the regrowth process I mentioned above.

Keeping Your Mind Sharp

Here are some strategies you can try to help you keep your mind sharp:

- Focus. Those senior moments are less about our brains turning to mush than they are a result of being distracted. Try to focus on the immediate task you wish to achieve, and eliminate all the excess activity going on in your brain.
- Make notes. If you write something down, it also helps you to remember it. You're thinking and seeing at the same time.
- Stay physically active. Exercise sends oxygen to the brain and can reduce the risk of some illnesses that lead to memory loss. Aerobic exercise is particularly good, so try to choose something that gets your blood pumping. It increases oxygen to your brain and reduces the risk for disorders that lead to memory loss, such as diabetes and cardiovascular disease. Exercise also enhances the effects of helpful brain chemicals and reduces stress hormones, lowers blood pressure, improves cholesterol levels, helps blood sugar balance, and reduces mental stress, all of which can help your brain as well as your heart.
- Be social. Hanging out with your friends and taking part in stimulating, fun conversations actually exercise your brain. Even going to a movie with a friend has cognitive benefits. I call that a win-win!
- Routine. Sometimes boring is good! If you always put your keys and glasses in the same place, you won't constantly be turning the house upside down looking for them. An additional benefit is that repetitive action creates a stronger memory.
- Sleep. A good night's sleep means your brain is getting the rest it needs.
- Keep learning by continuing to work, learning a new skill, or pursuing a new hobby. Your brain will be stimulated, and your memory will improve.
- Believe in yourself. Keep a positive, upbeat view of yourself. Don't keep telling yourself you're getting old and forgetful. That's a surefire way of becoming old and forgetful! If you believe in yourself, you'll achieve more.

- Save your brain. Why rack your brain trying to remember birthdays or which route to take to the airport? Take advantage of notebooks, calendars, and navigational systems in your phone and car. Save your brain for the important stuff that can't be done by a computer!
- Eat thoughtfully. Good nutrition is as important for your mind as it is for your body. A Mediterranean diet rich in olive oil, fish, vegetables, and fruit has proven to be beneficial.
- Avoid stress. A good way to ensure better mental health.
- Laughter is the best medicine. Spend time with fun people, and don't take yourself too seriously. When you get into a frustrating situation, laugh instead of rant!

Brain Games

If you don't use it, you lose it. We've all heard that before. Well, it certainly applies to the brain. The best brain exercises break your routine and challenge you to use and develop new brain pathways.

Here are some examples of brain games:

- Puzzles. Crosswords, sudoku, and math calculations all encourage mental dexterity. Jigsaw puzzles are another good brain game. Challenge yourself by trying new forms of puzzles. If you do sudoku every day and don't try anything different, your brain will eventually be less stimulated.
- Play strategy games. Scrabble, chess, and bridge are excellent strategy games that challenge the brain. You can play with friends or online.
- Break with routine. Drive home using a different route, walk round the market or store in a different direction (we all tend to follow the same route every time), or brush your teeth using the opposite hand. Surprisingly, these simple deviations from the normal routine stimulate the brain.
- Learn to play a musical instrument. Music taps into a different section of the brain from the areas we commonly use.

- Play the list game. When you're at the store with your shopping list, try to recall everything you need without referring to the list. Only look at it when you think you have everything you need in your basket. The more you do it, the more you'll remember.
- Do mental arithmetic. Try to do math in your head instead of using your calculator to work out every problem. Or if you're balancing your checkbook, why not try to do it the good, old-fashioned way with a pencil and paper?
- Cook. Trying new recipes uses almost all your senses, so stimulate several different areas of the brain. And if you're lucky, the results will taste great!
- Learn a foreign language. You don't have to aim for fluency, but try learning enough to understand the gist of a news broadcast or soap opera in your chosen language. If you're a keen cook, watching cooking shows in a foreign language makes learning fun. Alternatively, you can borrow courses from your local library, or do them online.
- Play the alphabet game in your head. See how many things beginning with a certain letter you can name. It can be anything from movie stars to books, movie titles, dog breeds, song titles, flowers, or anything you like. It's all brain exercise.
- Retrace a route in your mind. Think of a favorite walk, and try to recreate it mentally, remembering everything you saw on the way.
- Improve your fine motor skills. Fine motor skills utilize the smaller movements that occur in the wrists, hands, and fingers and require hand-eye coordination. Try something like drawing, knitting, model making, or scrapbooking.
- Join a dance class. Trying to remember the choreography is giving your brain a great workout while you exercise your body.
- Rethink reading. Of course, reading a book while curled up on your sofa is a good way to relax your body and stimulate your mind. However, try alternative ways of reading, like audiobooks, which involve a different sort of concentration. Or try reading a book you wouldn't normally have chosen. If you usually like reading chick lit, try a biography or historical novel for a change.

- Memorize. Try memorizing a poem, a speech, or a piece of prose.
- Take a walk. If you're feeling tired or you're having a midafternoon slump, go for a walk, or if that's not possible, try running on the spot for a few minutes. The movement will wake you up and make you feel refreshed.

So exercise your brain. It will literally make your second act unforgettable!

Chapter 26

QUOTES ON BEAUTY AND AGING FROM THE FAMOUS—AND THE AGELESS!

Have a sense of humor! When I inherited leadership of The 5th Dimension, I was so busy taking care of business and trying to see that things were perfect that I forgot to laugh! I had to learn to get my priorities in order (God, family, career) and not to take myself so seriously.

On the basis that smiling is the best facelift and laughter exercises your abs, here are a few quotes, some funny and some thought-provoking.

Lucille Ball

The secret of staying young is to live honestly,
eat slowly, and lie about your age.

Charles Schulz

Just remember, when you're over the hill, you begin to pick up speed.

Audrey Hepburn

For attractive lips, speak words of kindness—
For lovely eyes, seek out the good in people.
For a slim figure, share your food with the hungry.
For beautiful hair, let a child run his/her fingers through it once a day.
For poise, walk with the knowledge that you never walk alone.

Smokey Robinson

Beauty is spiritual. It exudes from the person
and doesn't have to be physical at all.

Betty Friedan

Aging is not "lost youth" but a new stage of opportunity and strength.

Iman

There are no beauty secrets.
Beauty is being comfortable and confident in your own skin.
We all have friends and loved ones who say 60's
the new 30. No. Sixty's the new 60.

David Bowie (Iman's husband)

Aging is an extraordinary process where you become
the person you always should have been.

George Bernard Shaw

We don't stop playing because we grow old. We
grow old because we stop playing.

Marilyn Monroe

A wise girl knows her limits. A smart girl knows that she has none.

Gloria Vanderbilt

The first thing to do is to start liking yourself and
having a feeling of self-esteem. If there's something
you really want to change, try to change it.

Diane von Furstenberg

My face carries all my memories. Why would I erase them?

Frank Lloyd Wright

The longer I live, the more beautiful life becomes.

Coco Chanel

Beauty begins the moment you decide to be yourself.
If you're sad, add more lipstick and attack.

Mark Twain

Wrinkles should merely indicate where smiles have been.

Sophia Loren

Nothing makes a woman more beautiful than
the belief that she is beautiful.
There is a fountain of youth: it is your mind, your talents, the
creativity you bring to your life and the lives of people you love.
When you learn to tap this source, you will truly have defeated age.

Oprah Winfrey

Every year should teach you something valuable; whether
you get the lesson is up to you. Every year brings you
closer to expressing your whole and healed self.

Sharon Stone

I have absolutely no objection to growing older. I am a stroke
survivor so I am extremely grateful to be aging—I have nothing
but gratitude for the passing years. I am aging—lucky, lucky me!

Ingrid Bergman

Getting old is like climbing a mountain; you get a
little out of breath, but the view is much better!

Chapter 27

LAST THOUGHTS

Advice is one of those things it is far more blessed to give than to receive!
—Carolyn Wells

The strange thing about age is it just creeps up on you. Suddenly you realize you're the same age as your mother was when you thought she was ancient!

All of us are looking for answers to this strange process of aging. I've tried to share the information that works for me. While we're obviously not all alike, there are certain common questions and problems relating to aging that we all address. I wanted to write a straightforward guide to being the best older version of yourself. I've spoken with friends and experts in all kinds of areas and tried to pass on the advice and tips I received and which I use myself.

The most important part of aging is health. If you're healthy, you feel well. If you feel good, you look good. If you look good, people react in a positive way to you. And when you're receiving positive vibes, you develop a sense of well-being.

My Advice to Young(er) People

The average person who will read books like this is probably well into her (his) thirties. It is best to start caring for the body and skin at an early age. It's not necessary to buy expensive creams and cosmetics. Just take preventive measures like using sunscreen and lotions and brushing and flossing your teeth (I know six-year-olds who already have cavities!), and continue good habits of cleanliness.

Many years ago, schools had health classes in which good hygiene was taught. Sadly this is not the case today. And many mothers and fathers don't think it is necessary or just don't take the time to teach their sons and daughters these important things!

> So I challenge you mature women to take it upon yourself to help our youth and any person you may observe not practicing good hygiene or improper dress or makeup. (Titus 2:3–5 NKJV)

It can be done in a palatable manner. I recommend you don't say, "You stink!"

I once had a friend tell me that I had bad breath. I'm glad he cared enough to tell me and that I didn't get angry with him, even though that's an embarrassing thing to be told. Upon going to the dentist, I discovered that the foul odor was caused by an abscess that would have gotten much worse and may have caused me to lose my tooth, had my friend not told me about my breath.

And Mature People

Keep growing. Remain teachable. Surround yourself with youthful (not necessarily young) people who care enough to tell you the truth about how you look and act, and receive their criticism with the love with which it is given while realizing that it is only their opinion. Do what you feel comfortable with. But remember if *everyone* tells you that hairstyle doesn't look good on you, give it a second thought!

I remember years ago when a dear friend came to Beverly Hills and wanted to go shopping at a well-known expensive store to celebrate her fiftieth birthday. She chose a dress she really liked and asked me how it looked. Now the dress was sleeveless, and she was not in the best shape. Her flabby arms did not look good at all, but I didn't want to hurt her feelings by telling her. Well, she bought the dress. If this happened today, I wouldn't mention her flabby arms, but I would suggest that the dress did not flatter her and suggest she select one with sleeves. She probably would have bought the sleeveless dress anyway, but at least I would have been honest with her. This incident happened over twenty years ago, and I *still* feel bad about not telling her the dress was not right for her. Oh well! I probably would have purchased the dress too. Like most of us, I have several items in my closet that I never should have bought.

And Finally

A longing fulfilled is sweet to the soul.
—Proverbs 13:19 (NKJV)

Lastly, I say to all those who, like I once was, are searching for themselves, "Remember, you are not lost! And it is never too late to start being the you that God meant for you to be—happy, healthy, and mentally, physically, and spiritually beautiful. Just learn to accept yourself as the wonderful being that God created. Also remember that stars may shine, but candles can also lead us out of the darkness. Go out and let your light shine! Here's to Grace in Your Second Act."

Love & Blessings,
Florence LaRue

ACKNOWLEDGMENTS

The older I get, the more I realize the truth of the statement, "One never reaches success alone!" I thank God for His timing and for putting the right people in my path. Without the constant encouragement of my many girlfriends over the last seven years, this book would still be in my head! I want to thank everyone who believed in me, which includes my son Geoffrey and my sisters Bernadette and Carlotta, who encouraged me to put my thoughts into writing. Many thanks also go to Cheryl Procter-Rogers and Deborah Pegues, who shared with me their wisdom and knowledge (although I was slow to act, thus delaying the publishing of this book!). I also thank my dear friends Minnie and Shirley, who encouraged me to follow my dream of writing a book; Dr. Joseph Canul, my chiropractor and encourager for over 40 years; Michelle and Scottie for their great suggestions for content and Ron Feuer for continually pushing me to finish it. Much appreciation and thanks go to Miles Robinson for tirelessly and patiently spending many hours with me to keep me on schedule and connecting me with my publisher and editor. Thanks to Jenny for all her hard work. And finally, I am grateful for my experience of over fifty years with my 5th_Dimension family, which provided the visibility and the platform for me to publish a book.

Printed in Great Britain
by Amazon

32148311R00111